Number Two
to
Tutu

I sought my God
My God I could not see.
I sought my soul
My soul eluded me.
I sought my brother
And I found all three.

*This is a Celtic prayer and, above it,
a Celtic design symbolising unity.*

Number Two
to
Tutu

A memoir

Michael Nuttall

Michael Nuttall

Cluster Publications
2003

ISBN 1–875053–34–4

First published in 2003.

Published by Cluster Publications
P.O. Box 2400
Pietermaritzburg
3200
Republic of South Africa

Typesetting by Justin James Advertising • Pietermaritzburg • South Africa
Printed by Interpak Books • Pietermaritzburg • South Africa

Contents

Foreword

Desmond Mpilo Tutu

This book demonstrates Michael Nuttall's gift for writing both simply and profoundly. He was reticent at first about the project because he did not want to draw attention to himself. Nor was I looking for an account that would be simply a tribute to me. Michael has aimed to achieve what he attractively calls a cameo of an extraordinary partnership between the two of us at a critical time in the life of our nation, South Africa.

It was in many ways a most unlikely partnership. As Michael explains in the book, we were both candidates for election as Archbishop of Cape Town, not only once but twice. While in the nature of things this could have come between us, we found ourselves drawn together instead. Differences of background, spirituality, race and culture were superseded and transformed.

At a practical level, as my deputy in the Anglican Church of the Province of Southern Africa, Michael relieved me of several responsibilities, thereby enabling me to fulfil my ministry in Southern Africa and in the wider world. Without this I would not have been able to pursue with the same vigour and energy the cause of justice and reconciliation for our country. I also often sounded him out on difficult decisions that I frequently had to make and always welcomed his advice.

I hope that this book will encourage many to consider that goodness is stronger than evil, love is stronger than hatred, light is stronger than darkness, life is stronger than death, and that God is all in all.

+ Desmond

Acknowledgements

Many have assisted, in their different ways, in helping me to fulfil this task, not least University College in the University of Durham for generously providing me with a Pemberton Visiting Fellowship for a term in 2001. Near University College stands Durham's great Norman cathedral, which houses the tombs of St Cuthbert the bishop and the Venerable Bede the historian. Their example brought ample inspiration to a retired bishop seeking to uncover an historical chapter of great moment in his faraway and much loved country. Desmond Tutu, I discovered, has the freedom of the city among his many awards, and this provided a further stimulus while writing this account in beautiful Durham.[1] I am grateful not only to the Master and Fellows of University College, but also to Paddy Kearney and Charles Yeats, friends and colleagues who, unknown to me, initiated and pursued the idea of this Fellowship.

Desmond himself has also encouraged this venture. I would not have embarked upon it without his support, and I am deeply grateful for his Foreword.

Several people have read the book in various stages of its draft form and have helped me with their comments and suggestions. Charles Yeats and Paddy Kearney were two of these. So were Bishop Stephen Sykes in Durham and Dr Vic Gatrell, Professor Christopher Brooke and the Revd Vanessa Herrick in Cambridge, where I was fortunate to spend a term in 2002 as Acting Dean of Gonville and Caius College. These overseas comments brought a valuable perspective from outside South Africa. Closer to hand, my historian son, Tim, and my brother, Jolyon, have provided particular help with their critique and advice. John Allen, who was Desmond Tutu's media secretary, has been very supportive from the beginning of this project. I am thankful to all these and others who have encouraged me to persevere.

My wife, Dorrie, has been unstinting with her encouragement and in her help with the typing of this book. During the time of the working relationship between Desmond and myself, our wives, Leah and Dorrie respectively, came to be described with affection as the 'Gogo' and 'Deputy Gogo' of the CPSA.[2] To them both this cameo – this witnessing to a story in which they shared – is dedicated with gratitude and love.

Endnotes

1   Desmond was told, to his great amusement, that the freedom of the city entitled him to set up a fruit and vegetable stall, free of charge, in the market place.

2   The word 'ugogo' means 'grandmother' in Zulu.

Photographic Credits

Cape Argus
Pages 12, 43

John Allen
Pages 48, 60, 73, 85, 88, 95, 97, 114

Sunday Tribune
Page 102

Crystelle Wilson
Page 120

Cape Times
Pages 151, 153

Dorrie Nuttall
Page 156

Setting the Scene

This book does not attempt to be an extensive analysis of the period of South African history it addresses. Nor is it a biography or an autobiography, though it has some features of both. It is in the nature of a memoir or a cameo. It provides glimpses of a human experience that invites contemplation in a divided and fractured world.

People have said to me from time to time that this story needs to be told. The telling of it involves vulnerability and this entails risk. Yet it is an important story touching themes of much significance for both church and state during a vital period of South African history: the varied roles of politicians and church leaders in a time of trauma and transition, the pursuit of justice and peace and the making of a costly reconciliation, the ordination of women, the nurturing of the church and its inner life, the seasoning of society with theology and prayer. My purpose is to explore, within that environment, the unfolding partnership between two individuals, Desmond Tutu and myself. Next to Pope John Paul II, Desmond was probably the best-known church leader in the world in the 1980s and 1990s. The book is in part a tribute to a remarkable man who was thrust by circumstances on to centre stage, both in our nation and in the world at large.

The purpose of this Prologue is firstly to make mention of our partnership and its essential quality, secondly to give a brief bibliographical note on some published work so far about Desmond Tutu, and finally and most substantially to provide an introductory insight into the dramatic political background against which our partnership in ministry and leadership took place.

Desmond Tutu led the Anglican Church in Southern Africa as its Archbishop from September 1986 to June 1996, a decade of remarkable challenge and change in the entire sub-continent. The official name of this church is the Church of the Province of Southern Africa (CPSA), whose founding bishop was Robert Gray, Bishop of Cape Town from 1847 to 1872.[1] The CPSA is international in the geographical area it covers, including South Africa and also Mozambique, Swaziland, Lesotho, Namibia, Angola and the islands of Saint Helena and Ascension.

From late 1989 until shortly after Tutu's retirement in 1996, I was Dean of the Province, which means the bishop next senior to the Archbishop. In addition to being Bishop of Natal, I became 'Number Two to Tutu', and an exhilarating and quite daunting partnership began. It soon developed into a close friendship. Indeed, I count it the highlight of my ministry as a bishop in South Africa over a period of twenty-four years to have had this special relationship with Desmond during the crucial period of our country's political transition beyond apartheid. Precisely because it was a partnership between a black archbishop and his white deputy, it presented a sign of healing and hope in our racially polarised and traumatised society. Some of the story's 'inside' features as well as the more obvious outward aspects are worth telling.

Shirley du Boulay's biography of Tutu ends at November 1987, just over a year into his decade as Archbishop of Cape Town.[2] In her Epilogue she wrote that it was too soon to assess his tenure of this high office.[3] Her book, published in 1988, could not envisage that Desmond would chair the South African Truth and Reconciliation Commission in the mid-1990s. These two decisive periods of his career have yet to be fully considered in a published account of his life. John Allen has given some hints on Tutu's time as Archbishop in his edited collection of some of Desmond's sermons and addresses from 1976 to 1994.[4] A collection of essays was published to mark Desmond's retirement as Archbishop in 1996.[5] Desmond himself in his *No Future Without Forgiveness* has written a profound account of the nature and work of the Truth and Reconciliation Commission, laced with many personal reflections and stories from his life. A full biography has yet to be written. This memoir is another foretaste, and it will perhaps whet the appetite for further studies and recollections.

The story told in this book occurred within a milestone chapter in South Africa's political history. The 1980s and early 1990s were years of deep national turmoil in a political struggle that threatened not simply to destabilise but to tear apart South African society. It became a struggle for human rights which caught the attention and the emotions of people around the world. The major protagonists were a powerful and determined apartheid state and an equally determined resistance movement both inside and outside the country.

The 'Soweto uprising' of 1976 marked the beginning of a major political and economic rupture.[6] 16 June 1976 was the day when the school children of Soweto said to the apartheid government 'Enough is enough', and the country was never to be the same again. It was essentially a peaceful protest of marching young people against an education policy that required them, though they were black children, to be taught in the medium of Afrikaans, the oppressor's language. It was savagely put down by police bullets, and the harrowing picture of Hector Peterson – the first child to be killed – being carried by his grieving sister and a friend, shocked the world.

At the risk of over-simplification, South African history since the 1600s could be described as a history of conquest and the eventual undoing of conquest. This is not the place to tell that chequered story, except to say that 16 June 1976 was the moment when the undoing of conquest took its most dramatic turn yet. It was followed by tens of thousands of young black South Africans taking to the streets in the country's major cities and confronting the security forces in their resistance to the harsh realities of apartheid. They were the torch-bearers of a new mobilisation after the relative quiesence of the 1960s which had followed the government's banning of the liberation movements. Soon they were joined by the emerging trade unions of black workers, who highlighted the growing urbanisation of black society, a socio-economic process which contradicted apartheid's attempt to foster rural 'homelands' instead for different tribal groups.

The government's response was a combination of repression and reform. Some saw this as an indication of the first steps away from apartheid. Others were more sceptical and interpreted the reforming strategies as an attempt to entrench apartheid in new ways. One of these strategies was to set up alliances with conservative black leaders in the so-called 'homelands' and in urban townships. This collaboration created a bitter site of struggle in the 1980s between these leaders and the representatives of protest politics who saw them as government stooges.

A high point of the government's divide-and-rule reform agenda was the inauguration in 1983 of a tri-cameral parliament through amendments to the South African Constitution, which hitherto had allowed only white citizens to sit in parliament. The intention was to attract conservative Coloured and Indian politicians, and the constituencies they represented, into a new-look parliament with three racially distinct chambers. Black Africans, who constituted the majority of the population, continued to be denied access to the heartland of state power. This divisive constitutional arrangement unleashed a new wave of civil conflict. The government and its satellites found themselves up against a newly created United Democratic Front (UDF), which was joined by hundreds of civic organisations as well as grassroots political groupings. Outside the country the African National Congress (ANC) strengthened its position and Umkhonto weSizwe,[7] its armed wing, extended its sabotage campaign.

Another phase of government repression was inevitable in the face of these challenges. Successive states of emergency were declared from 1985, lasting for the rest of that fraught decade. Tens of thousands of anti-apartheid

activists were detained without trial in a country-wide
clamp down, and South African Defence Force (SADF)
troops – most of them young conscripted white men – were
deployed in tense and volatile urban townships. The State
Security Council, rather than the Cabinet, dominated
national affairs in what was in effect a police state. By
1987 a stalemate had been reached in the South African
conflict. The government and its security forces remained
powerful enough to weaken and contain the resistance
movement, but not to crush it. The liberation
organisations were gathering in strength, but were not
powerful enough to topple the government. Their
leadership inside the country was severely weakened by
government bannings and arrests. Their stalwarts of the
1950s and 1960s, led by Oliver Tambo and Nelson
Mandela, were still in exile or in prison.

It is not easy to understand the complexity of events
which led to the breaking of the stalemate between 1987
and early 1990, but some significant pointers can be given.
It was precisely into this complexity that church leaders
sought to make a creative and decisive contribution. A
shifting balance of power occurred on both the national
and the international scene. Some military reverses in
Angola and the sheer cost of the war in South West Africa
(to become Namibia at its independence in 1990) began to
tell. International financial sanctions from 1986 touched
the government and the economy in a way that general
trade sanctions had failed to do because they were easily
circumvented. The collapse of Communism in Soviet
Russia and Eastern Europe in 1988-1989 was central to a
change of attitude in the South African government, which
had seen itself until then as a bastion of Christian
civilisation against the worldwide Communist threat, most
especially in Africa. Reformers in the government were
able to argue that the banned South African Communist
Party, a long-time and influential ally of the ANC, would be
significantly weakened by events in Eastern Europe and
Russia. Within South Africa popular opposition remained
resilient. The UDF was banned in 1988, but it regrouped
with the South African Congress of Trade Unions

(COSATU) to form the Mass Democratic Movement (MDM), which launched a series of huge freedom marches in the cities of South Africa during the latter part of 1989.

Clandestine meetings in Britain, from 1987 to 1990, between a group of Afrikaner academics and ANC exiles made a valuable contribution to the opening of new possibilities, especially since reports of these meetings went secretly to the President, who officially disapproved of any contact with the ANC.[8] Further meetings between white South African dissidents, representatives of big business and the ANC took place in Dakar and Lusaka. Within South Africa itself another drama was being played out, beginning in 1985 with the first of several encounters between Nelson Mandela and the Minister of Justice, Kobie Coetsee, leading to a secret meeting with the President himself in July 1989.[9] Both Mandela and the exiled leadership of the ANC were making it clear that they were open to a negotiated future for South Africa. While outwardly the overall situation seemed to be intractable in the late 1980s, events had occurred which, taken together, were bringing the impasse to an end.

When F W de Klerk succeeded P W Botha as State President in August 1989, the reform agenda of the government began to move more boldly in the direction of change. The first group of the Rivonia trialists, who had been sentenced to life imprisonment in the 1960s, were released from prison in October 1989. Finally, in February 1990, President de Klerk announced the unbanning of the liberation organisations, the intended rescinding of apartheid legislation and the imminent release of South Africa's most famous political prisoner, Nelson Mandela. The door to a negotiated political settlement for South Africa was thrown open.

Had De Klerk come to a definitive change of heart or were his moves a clever way to try to catch the ANC off guard and, through an intended new set of alignments with other minorities, to hold on to political power? This was one of the questions that had to be faced after the euphoria of February 1990 was over. The country entered into a highly unstable and violent, yet hopeful, phase of transition and negotiation. It was a time which elicited political heroism and magnanimity. It was also a period that saw intense conflict, opportunism, shifting alliances, distrust and trauma.

These were the circumstances, reaching from the turning point of 1976 to the first democratic elections of 1994, and indeed beyond this, in which church leaders found themselves called upon to be both prophets and pastors. From a later vantage point it is easy to think that the outcome of the South African conflict was a foregone conclusion. Part of Desmond Tutu's prophetic stance was always to proclaim that justice would prevail, even if at times this seemed to be an impossible dream. Yet there was no simple linear progression to the historic parliamentary elections of 1994. The patterns of conflict and their outcome were not predictable as different voices, tendencies and strategies operated on all sides of an intense human drama. The churches, woven as they are into the fabric of society, were intricately caught up in the unfolding events. The undoing of conquest was at issue. Desmond Tutu became a leading figure, with others, in the final process, both painful and exhilarating, of this undoing. Such a process is never a safe or easy option in the life of a nation, and it is a wonder – even a miracle – that we found a political solution at all. In certain respects – economic, social, psychological – the undoing of conquest is still continuing. All South Africans – 'black and white together', to use one of Tutu's favourite phrases – have a part to play in that wholesome transformation.

Prologue – Endnotes

1 The title 'Archbishop' first came into use during the time of Gray's successor, William West Jones.

2 Shirley du Boulay: *Tutu – Voice of the Voiceless* (Hodder and Stoughton, London et al, 1988).

3 Ibid, page 261.

4 John Allen (ed.): *The Rainbow People of God* (Doubleday, London et al, 1994).

5 Leonard Hulley, Louise Kretzchmar and Luke Lungile Pato (eds.): *Archbishop Tutu – Prophetic Witness in South Africa* (Human and Rousseau, Cape Town, 1996).

6 The word 'Soweto' is an abbreviation for South Western Township, a huge urban area south west of Johannesburg where many black African people, such as those who lived in Sophiatown, were forcibly moved in the apartheid era to conform with the policy of racially separate 'group areas'.

7 This term means 'Spear of the Nation' in Zulu.

8 See Allister Sparks: *Tomorrow is Another Country – the Inside Story of South Africa's Negotiated Revolution* (Struik, Johannesburg, 1994), pages 75-86.

9 See Allister Sparks: *Tomorrow is Another Country*, chapters 2-5. See also Nelson Mandela: *Long Walk to Freedom* (Macdonald Purnell, Randburg, 1994), pages 501-541.

The two candidates with Archdeacon David Nkwe. Some of the electors are in the background.

Chapter One

The Election of an Archbishop

"Hold on to your seats and enjoy the ride."
(Edward King, Dean of St George's Cathedral,
Cape Town)[1]

Desmond Tutu was elected on 14 April 1986 to be the
Anglican Archbishop of Cape Town. It was a momentous
day for him, for the church as a whole, for the nation and,
indeed, for the world. It was a poignant day for me too,
because I had been the other candidate in the election.

I was asked shortly after this historic election to write
an article about Desmond in the prestigious South African
magazine called *Leadership*. The writing of this piece was
an important catharsis for me. The editor of *Leadership*,
Hugh Murray, entitled the article "Soul Brothers", but
went on to state that 'it was Nuttall, as Bishop of Natal,
who posed the only serious alternative to the election of
Tutu. He was also the choice of the Anglican
establishment.'[2] How could the prophetic and
controversial Desmond Tutu and 'the choice of the
Anglican establishment' be 'soul brothers'?

The article included a picture of the two of us in a warm
greeting and embrace, together with the Archdeacon of
Johannesburg, David Nkwe, who later became the Bishop
of Klerksdorp. This photograph had been taken for the
Cape Argus during the morning tea break on the day of the
Elective Assembly. It tells a story of a good-humoured yet
wistful awareness of our predicament. Behind our relaxed
smiles lay an inevitable but hidden tension as some three
hundred clergy and lay representatives, together with the

bishops of the CPSA, were engaged in deciding our future that day. It is a fearful thing to fall into the hands of an elective assembly! We both remember the long hours as we sat together in the library of the Diocesan College (the church school popularly known as Bishops), sometimes talking quietly together, mostly keeping silent, as we awaited the outcome of the discussion and debate behind closed doors.

Desmond and I had known each other for over twenty years. We both began our ministry as bishops in 1976, he as Bishop of Lesotho and I as Bishop of Pretoria. This could not have been a more fateful time in South Africa, for it was the year of 'the Soweto uprising'. Though it was not completely obvious to us at the time, this resistance among young black South Africans was the turning of the tide in the demise of apartheid.

Desmond remained in Lesotho for only two years before returning to the turmoil of a South African based ministry. This was too short a period in Lesotho, but the times were out of joint and Desmond's fellow bishops agreed that he should come back to his home country. For the next seven years (1978 – 1984) he was General Secretary of the South African Council of Churches (SACC), which brought him into the forefront of a radical, ecumenical opposition to the Nationalist government and its apartheid policy. It was during these years that he became a well-known international figure, and his time with the SACC culminated with the award of the Nobel Peace Prize in 1984. Shortly thereafter he reverted to an Anglican diocesan ministry, this time in the key bishopric of Johannesburg.

I had, meanwhile, been Bishop of Pretoria from 1976 – 1981 which, looking back, were years of innocence and exposure in respect to much that was new and challenging for me. I had received no specific training for my new ministry and I found myself plunged into a huge part of the country with a diocese in which nine languages were used and which stretched northwards to the Zimbabwean border, westwards to Botswana and eastwards to Mozambique and Swaziland. Moreover, the city of Pretoria was (and still is) the administrative capital of the country. It was also the heartland of Afrikaner nationalism, which was in rampant power at the time. An early taste of this for me was an anonymous telephone call late on a Sunday night in June 1976, in which a gruff voice with a thick Afrikaans accent said: "If you carry on preaching like that, we will shoot you stone dead." This was in reaction to a gentle but firm commendation of racial integration which I had made in the course of my sermon earlier that evening at a Confirmation service where black and white young people were receiving the laying on of hands together. I had said: "Look around you here this evening for an answer to the needs of our traumatised country. It lies essentially in our willingness to come together." I did carry on preaching like that, and fortunately I have lived to tell the tale! In 1982 I was elected to be Bishop of Natal. It was painful and difficult to give up the Pretoria ministry and to leave the people I had come to know and appreciate there, but the move to Natal was in the nature of a homecoming, for it was there that I had been born and brought up. Yet the years that followed were far more than a homecoming. They became years of struggle and heartache in seeking to respond to the political conflict and violence in which our society became engulfed.

It was therefore a decade after we had embarked on our episcopal ministry, each in different ways, that Desmond and I found ourselves facing each other as candidates for the archbishopric of Cape Town. Ambition can be a subtle and unsuspected influence, and no doubt it exerted a certain pull on each of us, caught up as we were in the issues of both church and state. Yet neither Desmond nor I had any pressing personal desire to be Archbishop of Cape Town at that particular juncture in our life and work. I had been Bishop of Natal for only four years and had a strong sense of the need to stay there, quite apart from my commitment to the diocese as a born-and-bred Natalian. Desmond had much more recently become Bishop of Johannesburg. In his enthronement address in St Mary's Cathedral, Johannesburg on 3 February 1985 he had expressed himself plainly: "Unless it becomes abundantly clear that God wills me to do otherwise, I hope to end my active ministry as Bishop of Johannesburg."[3] Other people – including the Archbishop of Canterbury at that time, Robert Runcie [4] – did wish it to be otherwise. In the end, we were both prevailed upon to allow our names to be proposed. Our bread was cast upon the waters.

This was not the first time that we had made ourselves available for election in Cape Town. The same thing had happened at the preceding election in 1981. Desmond had been asked by Ted King, the redoubtable Dean of St George's Cathedral, to allow his name to be proposed. He had agreed, but in doing so had expressed the view, quaintly, that he didn't have 'a snowball's chance in hell' of being elected.[5] As it turned out, he received significant support, but not the two-thirds majority required for election. The same was true of myself. Indeed, none of the candidates, of whom there were several, received the required number of votes, and the decision was delegated to the Synod of Bishops. They chose their most senior member, Philip Russell, who was at that time the Bishop of Natal. Given his age, he would serve for a maximum of five years before moving into retirement (though the energy and enthusiasm for which he was well-known would ensure that this would be much more than a mere 'caretaker' ministry).

Those who wished to promote Desmond's candidature in 1986, knowing that he was a controversial figure in the eyes of many because of his strong prophetic stance against the South African government, realized the need to ensure, this time round, that he had much more than 'a snowball's chance in hell' of being elected. An element of canvassing on their part was inevitable, as indeed must have been the case around my name as well. This was a natural consequence of a democratic process. The institutional life of the church is not exempt from the strategic and tactical use of power. Immersed as it is in the social matrix, it would be foolish to pretend otherwise. This was all the more so when the CPSA was faced with the prospect of flying in the face of racist ideology and practice by choosing its first black Archbishop of Cape Town. It was an unsettling experience for me to be a possible foil to such a prospect.

Despite the human pressures, those who participated in the Cape Town Elective Assembly in 1986 were agreed that the hand of God was upon it in a special way. A consensus arose quickly and strongly. Even doubters became sensitive to the promptings of new possibility. The mystery of divine guidance was at work alongside human strategy. Desmond's caveat in St Mary's Cathedral, Johannesburg the previous year had come into play, for it *had* become abundantly clear that God wished him to do otherwise. In his brief acceptance speech to the Elective Assembly, he remarked: "I'm tongue-tied, and no doubt there are those who would prefer me to remain that way!" In the solemnity of the moment his well-known wit had not left him.

For Desmond's opponents in the Nationalist government and within white South African society, including some elements of the CPSA, his election was an unwelcome provocation. For his supporters it was a sign of hope and joy, with South Africa poised between two political intensities: greater oppression on the part of the government, and greater resistance on the part of the oppressed. Such a time in any nation is full of both peril and possibility. In facing both, the CPSA had made a bold and brave decision in electing Desmond to be its Archbishop.

Looking back now, I realize that this was my first experience of being 'Number Two to Tutu'. My prayer beforehand had been for 'a holy indifference' regarding the outcome of the election. Yet there came upon me immediately afterwards feelings of rejection that took me greatly by surprise. I too had been caught up in the power pressures and possibilities of the moment. The sense of rejection was a salutary experience, revealing a vulnerable humanity beneath the veneer of acceptance. When mind and emotion eventually became disentangled, I knew full well that Desmond's election was for all kinds of reasons the best thing that could have happened, both for me and, more importantly, for church and nation at that juncture of our history. My *Leadership* article enabled me to express this, and I ended it as follows: "This dynamic, diminutive man has made himself available because others asked that he should, to be a light in the darkness and to help lead us into the dawn of a new day. May he be given divine strength and wisdom for the task. His election to be Archbishop of Cape Town will be viewed by historians as a crossroads."[6] Desmond was good enough to telephone me when the article was published, to express appreciation for the generosity, as he described it, of my appraisal.

Were the new Archbishop and his runner-up yet 'soul brothers'? Not yet, I would say, but the phrase was prophetic because this is what we were to become.

In the three chapters that follow some insight will be given into the initial years of Desmond's time as Archbishop. This period culminated at the end of 1989 when, in a more direct and obvious way, I became his 'number two'. Our partnership began poignantly that year with a shared Christmas visit to the Holy Land and the historical origins of our faith. This is described in chapter five and is followed in the succeeding chapters by the main substance of our story.

One – Endnotes

1 These words, spoken to his Parish Council in April 1986, were quoted in the *Sunday Times Special Tribute* to Desmond Tutu, 26 November 2000.

2 *Leadership*, Volume 5, Number 4, 1986, page 124.

3 *Enthronement Charge of the Right Revd DM Tutu*, 3 February 1985, page 9.

4 Humphrey Carpenter: *Robert Runcie – the Reluctant Archbishop* (Hodder and Stoughton, London, 1996), pages 228-229. Runcie used his influence to secure the appointment of Timothy Bavin, Bishop of Johannesburg, as Bishop of Portsmouth in the Church of England, with the intention of clearing the way for Desmond Tutu to be elected to Johannesburg and subsequently, he hoped, to Cape Town. Terry Waite, his Assistant for Anglican Communion Affairs, described this as good diplomacy rather than intrigue.

5 Leonard Hulley, Louise Kretzschmar and Luke Lungile Pato (eds.): *Archbishop Tutu – Prophetic Witness in South Africa* (Human and Rousseau, Cape Town, 1996), page 26.

6 *Leadership*, Volume 5, Number 4, 1986, page 128. See Appendix One for this article in full.

Chapter Two

Building a Team

"I have seemed a good captain because it is easy
to lead a winning side.... I know I have made very
bad mistakes.... We have this treasure but in
earthenware vessels." (Desmond Tutu)[1]

As soon as Desmond became Archbishop he gave
himself to building a sense of teamwork around him. He
did this not only in his diocese of Cape Town, but also in
the CPSA as a whole and, in particular, among the bishops
of its seventeen dioceses.[2] Despite our shared vocation, the
bishops were a very mixed group in their theology, culture,
politics, race and temperament. One thing we had in
common was our masculinity, which prompted Desmond
to say to us once in a daring whisper: "Have you heard that
the most insecure of God's creatures is the human male?"
The question was amusing and also a searching one.
Could it be that some bishops tended to be authoritarian,
not simply because of their hierarchical standing in the
church but also because of an unacknowledged sense of
insecurity?

We bishops were encouraged to discover in Desmond's
time of leadership – through retreats and personal
reflection, through reading and conversation, through
arranged weekends for bishops and their wives, through
personal spiritual direction and guidance – the truth about
ourselves behind the purple we wore, the child within, the
more feminine traits, the authentic person. Out of this
there emerged a leadership more free to acknowledge

human frailty, to laugh or to cry, not to take ourselves too seriously. Desmond had taken the word 'liberation' as the theme for his tenure as Archbishop. Naturally, he was thinking primarily of the desperate need for political liberation in South Africa, but liberation is a concept with many faces. Unconsciously and spontaneously he brought a new and wholesome liberty into the lives of the other bishops around him and in their work together as a team. Yet it was a paradoxical liberty, for it brought with it a deeper dependence on the grace of God and on one another rather than on our own strength or status.

Desmond possesses a great capacity for affirming others, and one of the ways he showed this was through his letters. He is an avid writer of letters, especially personal letters. He would often, of necessity, delegate the answering of his massive public and official correspondence to a member of staff, usually giving an indication of the gist of his reply in his own hand at the top of the letter. More personal letters were his own special preserve, and he would constantly be writing them or, more accurately, scribbling them in his own, sometimes almost illegible handwriting. When he was young, Desmond contracted polio. This affected his right arm, leaving it slightly shorter and smaller than the other. He taught himself to write left-handed and has done so, a little clumsily, ever since.

There must be hundreds, if not thousands, of Desmond's personal letters treasured in private collections across the globe. I once observed him writing at least twenty-five 'thank you' postcards as I sat next to him on an aeroplane journey. He never omitted to say 'thank you'. His penchant for sending birthday or anniversary greetings, often accompanied by flowers, to all kinds of people became widely known and appreciated. He rarely failed to affirm or to reassure, even if he was in disagreement or pain with someone about something. There were, of course, also occasions in his official correspondence when he felt bound to rebuke or to criticise.

After his enthronement as Archbishop of Cape Town in

September 1986 the CPSA bishops each received a personal letter in which Desmond said:

"I am just writing to thank you very much indeed for caring so much that you put aside your very tight programme in order to be present to share with us in what was a truly magnificent occasion. I can say so because I had nothing to do with it – it was other people who worked like Trojans to ensure that we had this remarkable event.... I thank you very much for your love and your prayers and for your support. You know, more than I do, just how I need all of that. I shall need you, my dear brother, to help me be less horrible than I would otherwise be without all your help. I thank God for the fact that he has given you to me to be of assistance, and I know that I can depend on you. Please do not hesitate to speak your mind – I know that you do not need the encouragement, but I will be relying on you to speak the truth in love. It may hurt me sometimes but it is far better that we have an open and authentic relationship....Do remember that I am just the first among equals, and help me to be humble and to be one who knows that the first must be as the last, and that I should be binding a towel around my waist to wash the feet of my brothers. I need you very much." 3

Ten years later, at the time of his retirement, Desmond wrote again to his brother bishops:

"I am writing to you all in what is the last fortnight of my term as Archbishop. Quite unbelievable that it is nearly ten years since I was enthroned in Cape Town and the Church of God has survived that visitation. I used to say, trying to reassure whites about their survival under a black-led government, that if the CPSA could survive Tutu then they could be sure that they would not just survive but positively thrive in the new circumstances.

I am writing most inadequately to thank you most warmly for your love, prayers and support....You have carried me in all my weakness, my tears, my foibles, and helped to make my ministry happen.....If I have accomplished anything at all then it is we together who have accomplished it.

I think other church leaders envied our remarkable fellowship which helped to hold us together even when we differed fundamentally as over the issue of the ordination of women....Others envied the fact that you could say to the South African government over a threat to deal with me, 'If you touch him, you touch all of us', thereby forcing the regime to back off.

Thank you, thank you for it all and for more – for the hilarity of our meetings, for the tears, for the retreats, the Bible studies, the parties – thank you, thank you for allowing me for a while to be the headmaster."[4]

'The headmaster.' He gained that nickname because of his practice, in the free times during our regular meetings, of calling us to his room, one by one, so that he could find out how we were – 'in your heart', he would often say. How were our times of quiet, our retreat, our reading and days off, our holidays? Were we safeguarding these times? Were we looking after ourselves, and allowing God to do so, amidst all the heat and burden of the day in our ministry? Were we looking after our wives (if we were married) and our families? "How are you in your heart?" Then: "Let us have a little prayer together", and afterwards we would leave heartened or chastened, always deep in thought, a little embarrassed perhaps by our short session with 'the headmaster'. He once wrote a long and careful letter to each of the bishops about these self-same things in our lives. Pope John Paul II said to his biographer, George Wiegel: "They try to understand me from the outside. But

I can only be understood from the inside."[5] Desmond knew this truth as well about our human condition, and he did not want us to ignore it or forget it.

He was not only caring towards us personally; he was also building us into a team. The times through which we were living were abnormal and full of deep tension and challenge. The political crisis in South Africa was escalating all the time. The government began to make reforming sounds and yet imposed draconian states of emergency at the same time. Popular pressure for change gathered momentum, especially in the black townships. Economic sanctions and other forms of international pressure for change reached their peak.

The bishops were put to the test early in 1988 when President P W Botha went out of his way to demonise Desmond and to attempt to isolate him as an enemy of the state. An acrimonious correspondence took place between them, in which the finger-wagging Botha was in an aggressive and threatening mood. It seemed that he might impose a banning order on Desmond or take him into detention, as his government had done with many other opponents. The Bishop of Kimberley and Kuruman, George Swartz, in his capacity as Dean of the Province, called the bishops to an emergency consultation at a hotel near the Johannesburg airport. The Archbishop of Canterbury was also requested to send his personal emissary to this meeting, with the result that we had the Bishop of Lichfield, Keith Sutton, present with us. The sense of outrage and of solidarity with Desmond as our Archbishop was so strong that a clear message was sent to the President in which we said that if he touched Desmond he would touch us all. The result was twofold. The government did indeed back down, and we ourselves learnt an important lesson about the value of standing together in a prophetic witness.

I have in my possession one of Desmond's typical hand-written letters, sent two days after our emergency consultation. He wrote:

"My dear Michael

Thank you very much for your love, prayers and

support, especially over this interesting fortnight.
I am deeply touched and grateful. God bless you
and much love,
    +Desmond."[6]

I am sure that other bishops must have received similar
letters. The refrain is one of gratitude for love, prayer and
support. The last two were very important to him, but the
first was the greatest of all. Desmond often spoke of how
he loved to be loved. It was a need which he was denied all
too often in his own country by those who were intensely
hostile to his prophetic stand against apartheid. He
himself has wondered at times whether this need was a
sign of weakness, an indication of too great a dependency
on affirmation and affection. In a newspaper interview in
April 2001 he was asked: "What do you think now are your
weaknesses, your frailties?" Desmond replied: "I have a
very strong weakness for being liked. I want to be popular.
I love to be loved. One has enjoyed the limelight. I am
guilty of the sin of pride. Sometimes I find it very difficult
to be humble – that is why it is so good to have Leah. She
pulls me down a peg or two. To her I'm not an archbishop
with a Nobel Prize; I'm just a not-very-good husband who
likes gardens but won't do any gardening."[7] Not many
church leaders are as transparent as that.

The positive side of Desmond's acknowledged weakness
was that it made him acutely conscious of the need to love
and affirm other people. This was the secret of his team
building, and it had an added importance in the difficult
and testing times through which we were living politically
in Southern Africa. Love, prayer and support for one
another became cardinal virtues for such a time.

Two – Endnotes

1   *The Archbishop's Charge to Provincial Synod*, Kimberley,
    September 1995, page 8.

2   This number was to increase to twenty-two by 1990 as the
    result of multiplication in three dioceses (Johannesburg,
    Pretoria and St John's). Angola was added as an
    embryonic completely new diocese in 1995.

3   Letter to me, 23 September 1986.

4   Letter to me, 20 June 1996.

5   George Wiegel: *Spiritual Stars of the Millennium* in *The
    Tablet*, 23/30 December 2000.

6   Letter to me, 24 March 1988.

7   Gyles Brandreth's interview with Desmond called *My Idea
    of Heaven* in *The Sunday Telegraph*, United Kingdom,
    15 April 2001.

Chapter Three

Facing Differences

"There may be moments even in a statesman's life when wisdom is not the first quality in demand, but when what a moral situation needs is an explosion and let wisdom be damned." (Owen Chadwick)[1]

Owen Chadwick, the renowned English historian, was writing about Pope Pius XII and the controversy surrounding his failure to make a resounding condemnation of the Nazi persecution of Jews. Pope Pius was a shy, otherworldly person with a hesitant nature, and this made bold decisions difficult for him. Yet, in the face of the mounting evidence on the Holocaust, there was no excuse for silence or even for a guarded critique. "It is wise to think before one speaks," Chadwick writes, "it is very wise to think deeply before one speaks, but there are moments in history when it is better just to speak without thinking."[2]

There were moments when Desmond spoke without thinking, as when, during his brief spell as Bishop of Johannesburg (1985-1986), he blurted out in a moment of exasperation to a newspaper reporter: "America and the West can go to hell!"[3] This was in response to a speech by President Ronald Reagan expressing opposition, as had the British Prime Minister, Margaret Thatcher, to economic sanctions against South Africa. It was not the kind of comment one expected to hear from a church leader. Indeed, there were those who were shocked and angered by it, especially the supporters of the Reagan and Thatcher policy of 'constructive engagement' with the Afrikaner Nationalist government in South Africa. How can you engage constructively, Desmond would have retorted, with a government that perpetuates an immoral, un-Christian and evil policy of racial separation and oppression? This was a policy not to be reformed, but eradicated, root and branch.

It is not that Desmond is incapable of careful thought: far from it. His mind was always sharp and his reasoning deep. But, like Jeremiah in the Bible, he had a fire within him which made silence in the face of evil unbearable.[4] He explained this on a telling occasion in 1982. This was when the South African Council of Churches, which he then led as its General Secretary, was being investigated by the government-appointed Eloff Commission of Enquiry.

> "There is nothing the government can do to me that will stop me from being involved in what I believe is what God wants me to do. I do not do it because I like doing it.... I cannot help it when I see injustice, I cannot keep quiet. I will not keep quiet, for, as Jeremiah says, when I try to keep quiet, God's word burns like a fire in my breast. But what is it that they can ultimately do? The most awful thing that they can do is to kill me, and death is not the worst thing that can happen to a Christian."[5]

A fiery prophet at the SACC was one thing, for it was supremely a social justice agency and it could therefore the more easily accommodate, and indeed welcome, the prophet as its leader. Such a person within the structures of a church denomination is another thing altogether, because of the variety of emphases and priorities – and people – it embraces. Beyers Naude, the distinguished Dutch Reformed leader who became a trenchant critic of apartheid, was driven out of the ministry of his denomination, but was hailed as a hero by the SACC.

There were some who wanted Desmond Tutu driven out as well. Instead, he was chosen as the next Archbishop! An important difference was that Beyers Naude's church was white and Afrikaner, and it had spawned apartheid with what it considered to be a theological justification for racial separation. The CPSA consisted of black and white together and had officially resisted apartheid from the beginning. Desmond's election was nonetheless a remarkable development, a sign that the church was ready to take a dramatic step forward in that resistance.

As the next tumultuous decade began to unfold, it became clear that there were differences to be faced, even among the bishops, as well as solidarities to savour. In his first letter to the bishops Desmond had acknowledged that this would be so: "Please do not hesitate to speak your mind.... It may hurt me sometimes but it is far better that we have an open and authentic relationship."[6] It was not easy to follow this advice. Who of us would want to cause hurt, and which of us was not sometimes overwhelmed by the strong views and the sheer presence of this world-acclaimed figure at the helm? Silence was an easier option, or that respectful, even fearful, deference to authority so well attested within the life of the church. Subconsciously we were faced with an intriguing question: how does one relate to a leader who has the world at his feet, or more subtly, how does one respond to the mystique of the prophet and the prophet's actions or utterances?

On the political front, one of the most burning issues we had to face in the first years of Desmond's archiepiscopate was whether or not to support economic sanctions against an intransigent South African government. Shortly before he became Archbishop, Desmond had made a call on his own initiative for comprehensive punitive sanctions. He had earlier given the government warning that he would be compelled to do this unless, within twelve to eighteen months, significant changes were introduced. The bishops, as well as the church at large, were deeply divided on this question. At his enthronement as Archbishop, Desmond had welcomed his brother bishops of the CPSA, and had said: "You are embarking on the thankless task of trying to keep your Metropolitan in check, not to do or say too many outrageous things."[7] His 'outrageous' call for international sanctions seemed to many to be precisely an example of a fiery explosion, and let wisdom be damned. Yet the timing was very thoughtfully and deliberately planned. Desmond felt that it was important to make his call before the Cape Town Elective Assembly, so that if he were elected as archbishop, those responsible would have done it with their eyes wide open. He therefore chose 2 April 1986 – just twelve days before the Elective Assembly – joking afterwards that 1 April would hardly have been an auspicious date.

The bishops did not settle for the easy solution of simply agreeing to differ. Instead, we wrestled together with the question and set up a series of consultations with experts in economics to inform ourselves and to consider every aspect. Desmond himself had made his bold stand, yet he did not attempt to bulldoze his fellow bishops into supporting it, welcome though such immediate support would obviously have been. He waited and participated himself in the consultative process. Together, we walked the road of a careful wisdom! In the end we came to an agreement which involved give-and-take on all sides. The Synod of Bishops expressed their mind in favour of specific targeted pressures rather than indiscriminate comprehensive sanctions. We said in our statement of December, 1988: "We believe that the imposition of carefully selected and specifically targeted forms of pressure, including economic and diplomatic pressure, holds potential to bring about relatively rapid change."[8] We also added a cautionary note. "We recognise the moral dilemmas which the advocacy of pressure can create for us, and we approach this issue with pastoral concern for all the people of Southern Africa. In our understanding of ethical issues, means are important as well as ends. In the South African context we would wish to choose forms of action which will avoid as far as possible the creation of further unemployment."[9]

Before making a public call for these pressures, we invited comment from the membership of our church. In

June 1989, the debate was taken into the Provincial Synod which is the CPSA's highest court, consisting of lay and clerical representatives as well as the bishops. The Synod declared that there was indeed a need for selective economic sanctions to be investigated.[10] So it was that the focus narrowed down to financial sanctions in particular. While even these had their own peculiar complexities, it was considered that they would be swiftly effective as a pressure on the South African government, whereas general trade sanctions were easily circumvented. In addition, financial sanctions, such as a refusal to offer new loans or to reschedule existing ones, would impact directly on the government and only indirectly on the population as a whole. Desmond was in Oslo in July 1989. He was quoted as saying: "The state of emergency, the death squads and the criminalisation of political activity make our situation difficult, but our people are in good spirits and apartheid will be ended. We need the world's help to bring the apartheid regime to the negotiating table. From now on banking and loan sanctions must be applied. Foreign loans must not be granted without conditions."[11]

The process we had gone through was a notable example of teamwork on a sensitive and emotive subject. Everyone made adjustments in opinion, including the Archbishop. We were painfully aware that there were some, especially among white South Africans, though they included also black leaders such as Mangosuthu Buthelezi,[12] who saw our stance as a great betrayal. Some members of our church reacted with their own form of sanction by ceasing their financial contributions to their church. We bore the critique even of that great liberal champion of human freedom, Alan Paton, who in his eighties wrote in the closing pages of his autobiography: "I hope our country will pull itself out of its present mess, and that the best and the wisest of our people will shape our new society. I take it for granted that our future has become the concern of many of the governments and the ordinary people of the world. They have every right to concern themselves and to bring pressure to bear upon us. I believe they are utterly mistaken to think that sanctions and disinvestment will bring beneficial change. You cannot change society for the better by damaging or destroying its economy."[13]

Robert Runcie, Archbishop of Canterbury, put the matter aptly when he preached at an open-air Eucharist on the day of Desmond's inauguration as Archbishop of Cape Town. "A person precariously balanced on top of a pile of logs is aware of the hurt that will be done if it collapses. Not surprisingly he calls for stability, for change that is gentle. A person who is squeezed under the pile of logs is conscious of his present pain. He calls out to be freed, even if it brings down the whole pile."[14] Desmond, conscious in particular of those under the pile, had made his prophetic call. Subsequently, this call was more specifically focussed in the light of further enquiry and discussion. In principle, the bishops were all of one mind with a shared and underlying conviction about the evil of apartheid and the need for it to be removed urgently and finally and preferably by non-violent means.

The process I have been describing took three years to complete, amidst many other activities in which the bishops were fully engaged. It took place at a crucial time in the life of South Africa, when suffering and violence were rife and fundamental change was critically needed if the nation was not to slide from a low-intensity civil war into a much more serious civil conflict. Did we take too long to reach a conclusion? Was this a telling example of episcopal fiddling while our Rome burned? Desmond must have been tempted at times to think so, though he had the satisfaction of knowing that he had made his stand already and was in a sense waiting for his fellow bishops to catch up with him. He understood both the value and the pitfalls of caution and commented on this in a personal letter to me in October 1988: "I am sure we need your cautious approach, particularly your Metropolitan who can act too precipitately, though I think that it was Bonhoeffer who warned that it might be better to act in a difficult situation even if that action turned out to be wrong, than not do anything for fear of acting wrongly."[15] Dietrich Bonhoeffer, famous for his courageous opposition as a Christian to the Nazi government in the Germany of his day, had concluded that it was ethically acceptable even to participate in an assassination plot against Adolf Hitler with a view to bringing the war and Hitler's evil policies to an end. It cost him his life.

Were we too cautious on the sanctions question? Were we too consultative, whether of the church at large or of the economic experts, too diffident to say plainly 'Thus saith the Lord'? There is an unnecessary caution and there is one based on the awareness of complexity. No doubt both were present, but the complexity of the question was, I think, the primary stumbling block. The broad consensus we reached in the end was based upon a well-informed conscience. At the same time it was important to be reminded that an overdose of caution or meticulousness of mind, for all its useful value, can be a hindrance, especially in situations of grave injustice where a brave boldness is required. Indeed, it can even induce a moral failure to act when action is required, and what can be worse than that?

Three – Endnotes

1   Owen Chadwick: *Pius XII – the Legends and the Truth* in *The Tablet*, 28 March 1998.

2   Ibid.

3   See Shirley du Boulay: *Tutu – Voice of the Voiceless* (Hodder and Stoughton, London et al, 1988), page 252.

4   See Jeremiah 20: 9.

5   *The Divine Intention: Presentation by Bishop D Tutu, General Secretary of the South African Council of Churches, to the Eloff Commission of Enquiry on 1st September 1982* (S A Council of Churches, Braamfontein, no date), page 35.

6   Letter to the bishops, 23 September 1986.

7   *Enthronement Charge of Archbishop Desmond Tutu*, 7 September 1986, page 2.

8   *Statement by the Synod of Bishops of the Church of the Province of Southern Africa*, 4 December 1988.

9   Ibid.

10 *Acts and Resolutions of Provincial Synod, 1989*, pages 53-54.

11 *Bishopscourt Update*, 15 July 1989.

12 Buthelezi was the Chief Minister of the 'homeland' of KwaZulu and a lay member of the CPSA.

13 Alan Paton: *Journey Continued* (David Philip, Cape Town, 1988), page 301. Paton was also an Anglican and had been admitted to the Order of Simon of Cyrene, a group of lay men and women in the CPSA honoured by the Archbishop of Cape Town for their distinguished service and witness.

14 *A Sermon Preached by the Archbishop of Canterbury, Dr Robert Runcie, at a Concelebrated Eucharist held in the Goodwood Stadium, Cape Town*, 7 September 1986, page 5.

15 Letter to me, 25 October 1988.

Chapter Four

Principle, Protest and Pressure

"There were times when you had to whistle in the dark to keep your morale up, and you wanted to whisper in God's ear: 'God, we know you are in charge, but can't you make it a little more obvious?'" (Desmond Tutu)[1]

Politically speaking, Desmond's ten years as Archbishop fell into two major segments. The first was from 1986-1990, when the politics of repression on the one hand and of resistance on the other reached their zenith. The second was from 1990-1996 which were the years of major and even miraculous political transition. Paradoxically the first phase occurred just when the apartheid regime was beginning to speak the language of reform. This is exactly the time when the body politic becomes most restless and demanding, while those in authority, despite their harsh and dictatorial actions, are actually at their most vulnerable. A new South Africa was inexorably coming to birth amidst much pain and travail. For our country the darkest hour was the one before the dawn.

In 1990 there came the breakthrough with President F W de Klerk's famous speech in Parliament on 2 February when he lifted the ban on the African National Congress and all other banned organizations, and announced that Nelson Mandela was to be freed unconditionally. On 10 February, the day before Mandela's release, Desmond was asked how he felt. "We are all just exuberant," he replied. "We've been praying, working and campaigning for this release and we are on Cloud Nine because I am quite certain myself that now negotiations are going to get under way, and he is going to be a very crucial factor in making them come to a successful conclusion."[2]   These were prophetic words, but the negotiation process took far longer than we originally hoped it would. Indeed, the years leading up to the first free democratic elections on 27 April 1994 were as turbulent and dangerous as the period that had preceded them. Many times we were on the brink of despair, but in the end hope prevailed and the new day did dawn. The long and patient queues of voting South Africans, black and white together for the first time, confounded all the prophets of doom, while the inauguration of Nelson Mandela as President on 10 May 1994 held not only South Africa but the whole world in thrall.

Finally, these two segments of our political history were brought together in a most remarkable way when Desmond was asked by President Mandela to chair the newly established Truth and Reconciliation Commission. This would involve looking back into the brutal and painful past in a search for healing of the many wounds. It was a task so demanding and so delicate that Desmond needed to draw on all the deepest resources of mind, heart and inner strength to fulfil it. He became, par excellence, the wounded healer. This work carried him into the period beyond his retirement as Archbishop in June 1996, but it began in December 1995 as the coping-stone of all that he had sought to build, in both church and nation, during the preceding years.

We return to 1989, a mid-point in the saga of this extraordinary decade. This was the year when the bishops of the CPSA finally reached consensus on the subject of economic sanctions by the international community. It was the year of mounting resistance internally to the South African government. In the previous year the government had attempted to reassert its control by outlawing no less than seventeen anti-apartheid organizations, notably the United Democratic Front (UDF) which since its formation in 1983 had become the most significant focus of popular resistance within the country. Alternatives soon arose. The South African Council of Churches resolved to launch its 'Standing for the Truth' campaign, which committed itself to non-violent direct action. Early in the morning of 31 August 1988 its headquarters (Khotso House, meaning 'House of Peace') in Johannesburg were bombed. It later emerged, through testimony to the Truth and Reconciliation Commission by the Minister of Law and Order at that time, Adriaan Vlok, that this had been done on the instructions of President P W Botha himself. Early in 1989 the restricted leadership of the UDF reconstituted itself into a loosely structured Mass Democratic Movement (MDM).

Meanwhile, a simultaneous crisis arose at leadership level in the government. As a result of a stroke President Botha resigned the leadership of the National Party while remaining State President. F W de Klerk was elected as his successor on 2 February, exactly a year before his epoch-making speech in Parliament in 1990. In the months that followed an awkward situation of dual leadership became ultimately unworkable, and Botha's irascibility towards even his closest colleagues was increasingly intolerable. On 14 August, under pressure from the Cabinet, he decided petulantly to stand down, and De Klerk succeeded him as President of South Africa.[3]

A parliamentary election – the last one, so it turned out, for the white electorate alone – was due to be held on 6 September, and this placed a huge onus of responsibility on the new President. At the same time the defiance campaign was reaching a crescendo, particularly in Cape Town, the seat of parliamentary government. Police violence against protesting people was unrestrained and brutal, culminating on the day of the election when over twenty people were killed in Cape Town's townships. A member of the police, Lieutenant Gregory Rockman, was so appalled that he courageously gave a press interview denouncing the behaviour of the so-called riot squad as being like that of 'wild dogs'.

The following day, 7 September, became a landmark day in Desmond's career and vocation. Once again the fire burned in his breast, or more accurately, a well of tears arose within him. John Allen, his media secretary, tells what happened:

> "On the evening of 7 September, Tutu was told that reports were circulating that the previous day's death toll was much higher than so far revealed. He broke down weeping and went to his chapel. He spent the evening alone and slept badly. The following morning he told Matt Esau, his personal assistant at the time, that he wanted to call for a protest march the following Monday. But Esau appealed for more time for planning, and the date was set for Wednesday 13 September....No-one knew what support there would be, but by the time Tutu arrived at the cathedral it was packed and thousands of people filled the surrounding streets. In a spectacle not seen in South Africa since the banning of the ANC and the PAC nearly thirty years before, a crowd estimated by most newspapers at 30,000 moved triumphantly through the city to the City Hall." [4]

This Cape Town event and its origin were an illuminating demonstration of the prophet in action. Desmond had consulted no one. He had not formed a committee or made a strategic plan. He had simply announced a decision, born of his own anguish and prayer; he would be leading a protest march. His chaplain, Christopher Ahrends, commented later that it was as if the decision "had dropped out of heaven."[5] It was also earthed in the Archbishop's awareness of a city in crisis. He touched a raw nerve and people responded spontaneously in their thousands.

President de Klerk, under pressure from diplomats and others, had decided at the last moment, against the strong opinions of some of his security advisers, to allow the march to take place. It would otherwise have been illegal under the long-continuing state of emergency regulations. This in itself indicates the courage implicit in Desmond's decision to have the march and to lead it. The success of this popular protest opened the door to similar marches in other major cities in South Africa. Indeed, there are grounds for seeing a connection between these South African protest marches and those which erupted later that same year in Eastern Europe. Desmond himself commented gleefully: "We marched in Cape Town and the Berlin Wall fell down!" Who can tell how one event can affect others in our global village?

Certainly these massive signs of popular pressure for peaceful change were a crucial factor in the unfolding political events in South Africa. I remember vividly the sense of expectation, together with an unusually strong peace of mind, with which I participated in the huge march in Durban on 22 September. The leadership of the MDM wanted the church leaders to be at its front in order to give it respectability! We had our own reasons for leading 20,000 people through the streets of Durban on that day. Later I did my best to express some of these in my regular monthly newsletter to the people of the diocese of Natal. I wrote:

"We live in an abnormally unjust society. So far as I am aware, ours is the only society left in the world which actually legislates for racial discrimination. That is what makes the Republic of South Africa so notoriously unique....No amount of rhetoric on the part of apologists for the Republic can gainsay that fact....

The church has no alternative but to raise its voice in protest against such a state of affairs, because apartheid is a sin against God....Racial discrimination is a sin against God because it is a sin against God's creatures, made in his image and redeemed by his Son at great cost. Ever since 1948, and before, our church and other churches have made this conviction known. Some have described this as 'interference in politics'. The truth is that politicians have interfered with a

God-given order for his creation, and the church would have lost her soul had she not objected on God's behalf.

Normally, in situations of socio-political injustice, the church, in making her response, will confine herself to issues of moral principle. She will give a theological reason, as I have done above, for judging a policy or system to be morally wrong. The church will not normally engage in specific strategies for change, though individual Christians are, of course, always free to do so.

But what happens in a situation like ours of profound and long-continuing injustice which, in one over-riding respect, is uniquely offensive to the rest of the world community and, more seriously, to God? In such situations one should expect unusual responses. Statements of moral principle will not be enough. They will be accompanied, albeit reluctantly perhaps, by actions of protest and pressure....The church will always by preference choose the non-violent option; but this will not mean a mere folding of the hands and doing nothing.

It is against this background that you have seen bishops of the church, with others in leadership positions (including a courageous mayor in Cape Town), taking to the streets or beaches[6] in solemn protest.... Friday, 22 September was, in fact, for me an extraordinary day. It will be etched in my memory for a long time to come...." [7]

I concluded my remarks with a final point that sought to put the protest march into another perspective.

"One last point. Alongside such stirring events, inevitably controversial as with some of the things Jesus was involved in, the everyday life and ministry of the church continues. That is as it should be. Do not make the mistake of thinking that bishops spend their time on little more than protest and pressure. In addition that week I attended a clergy retreat, conducted two confirmations, visited a sick priest, tried to respond creatively to two serious pastoral crises in the diocese, attended to inevitable correspondence and interviews, and went to a 21st birthday party for the elder daughter of one of our clergy. I even managed to fit in an afternoon jog! Life is full – and interesting!"[8]

After he had read my exposition, Desmond once again sent a hand-written postcard. It was very brief but it conveyed a great deal.

"My dear Michael
I found your 'apologia' for principle, protest and pressure very good. Well done as always. Much love to you and Dorrie. God bless you.
+Desmond."[9]

In the middle of this tumultuous year another highly significant event had taken place about which neither of us was aware. On 5 July a secret meeting occurred at Tuynhuys, the presidential residence in Cape Town, between President P W Botha and the government's prisoner of twenty-seven years, Nelson Mandela. Mandela had been pressing for such a meeting for several years on the grounds that he believed the time had come for political negotiations between the government, the ANC and others to begin. Botha, in his turn, was unwilling to release Mandela unless he first renounced the use of violence in the pursuit of political change. This Mandela refused to do, with the result that there was a stalemate. But that inter-personal meeting, conducted as we now know in a courteous spirit, was a sign amidst all the horror of that time of inevitable change yet to come. Nelson Mandela, in his autobiography, wrote of the incident as follows: "While the meeting was not a breakthrough in terms of negotiations, it was one in another sense. Mr

Botha had long talked about the need to cross the
Rubicon, but he never did it himself until that morning at
Tuynhuys. Now, I felt, there was no turning back."[10]

At the Synod of Bishops, meeting in Cape Town in
November 1989, the Dean of the Province, George Swartz,
Bishop of Kimberley and Kuruman, felt a need to stand
down because of pressure of work and some ill health. I
was elected by the bishops to succeed him. This was an
awesome moment for me, the full import of which dawned
on me only in the years that followed. South Africa
politically was at a crossroads. Here was a black South
African Archbishop with a white South African deputy:
could this intriguing partnership become an icon of hope
and possibility in a divided nation on the eve of its
transformation?

*On the day of my election as Dean of the Province
in November 1989*

Four – Endnotes

1   John Allen (ed.): *The Essential Desmond Tutu* (David Philip, Cape Town, 1999), page 57.

2   Desmond Tutu: *The Rainbow People of God* (edited by John Allen), (Doubleday, London et al, 1994), pages 186-187.

3   See FW de Klerk: *The Last Trek – a New Beginning* (Macmillan, 1999), chapter 13.

4   Desmond Tutu: *The Rainbow People of God* (Doubleday, London et al, 1994), pages 180-181.

5   See Paul Bell: *The Retirement of Archbishop Tutu* in *A Tribute to Archbishop Desmond Tutu – Spiritual Father of the Rainbow Nation* (1996).

6   There were also protesting presences on 'whites only' beaches at that time. Desmond participated in these as well.

7   *Bishops' Newsletter*, Diocese of Natal, November 1989. For a further account of this and other events of that period, see Michael Nuttall: *Living Through Heady Times* in Anthony M Gamley (ed.): *Denis Hurley – a Portrait by Friends* (Cluster Publications, Pietermaritzburg, 2001), pages 148-151.

8   *Bishops' Newsletter*, Diocese of Natal, November 1989.

9   Postcard to me, undated.

10 Nelson Mandela: *Long Walk to Freedom* (Macdonald Purnell, 1994), page 540.

Chapter Five

Pilgrims to the Holy Land

"A visitor to Israel today who takes the trouble to visit both the cosmopolitan and historic centres of Tel Aviv and Jerusalem as well as the captive degradation of the Gaza strip cannot but think of the rottenest days of South Africa." (The Guardian)[1]

The first public thing Desmond and I did together in our new roles was not in South Africa but in Israel/Palestine, the Holy Land. He had been invited in June 1989 by the Anglican Bishop in Jerusalem, Samir Kafity, to undertake a pastoral visit there of witness and peace during the Christmas period. He invited me to accompany him, neither of us knowing at that stage that, when Christmas came, I would be the bishop next senior to him in the CPSA. We were joined by two of his staff members, Canon Winston Ndungane, his Executive Officer and seven years later to become his successor as Archbishop of Cape Town, and John Allen his media secretary. As we flew out from Johannesburg to Frankfurt and then to Tel Aviv, the thought of Christmas in Jerusalem and Bethlehem, while it would separate us sadly from our families, brought with it a sense of joyful anticipation. In the event, the joy was mixed with a great deal of pain and sorrow, for we found ourselves in a political situation uncannily similar to our own.

The first 'intifada' (meaning 'uprising') by Palestinians

against Israel's 1967 occupation of the West Bank and Gaza had begun. On Christmas Eve we had a vivid taste of what was going on in the Holy Land. Bishop Kafity and other church colleagues had arranged for an afternoon Carol Service at the Shepherds' Field, where according to tradition the angels sang to the shepherds on the first Christmas Eve. This was just outside the town of Beit Sahour. The Palestinian townspeople of Beit Sahour had recently decided to withhold payment of taxes to the Israeli government on the principle of 'no taxation without representation'. Israel's reaction to these voteless people was swift and severe. Troops came to confiscate their property in lieu of taxes. We were told this story as we were driven through Beit Sahour on our way to the Carol Service. We wondered why the town was deserted. When we arrived at Shepherds' Field we discovered the answer. People were there in their thousands to hear the well-known Archbishop from South Africa and to express their solidarity with one another. Desmond was mobbed and greeted as a hero. There was also a large military presence, with Israeli soldiers completely encircling the huge crowd. We were caught in the middle of the tension and anguish of Israel/Palestine, which to this day remains unresolved.

We were also aware that we were standing on holy ground, very near the historical origins of our faith. Representatives of what Samir Kafity described as 'the three Abrahamic faiths' (Jew, Christian and Muslim) were present. The atmosphere, though tense and fragile, was one of dignity, restraint, laughter and welcome. I wondered how Desmond would handle the situation as he rose to speak. He expressed gratitude for their welcome and hospitality. Then, shrewdly, he simply began to tell them about South Africa. He spoke about popular non-violent resistance to oppression in his home country and about the rising tide of hope for change against all the odds. His audience were not fools; they made the comparison, and perhaps the contrast, immediately. Then Desmond spoke about the inalienable divine gift of human dignity set forth in the birth of Christ when God took upon himself our human flesh. Those present were riveted and inspired, and a tense crowd dispersed peacefully when it was all over.

Later that evening it was my turn to preach, this time to a very different and much smaller congregation gathered under a starlit sky on the roof of the church of the Holy Nativity in Bethlehem. I spoke about the Christian journey, whether short or long, and about wounded pilgrims bruised by the events of their time, and about faith in the bright Morning Star, the Christ Child as the source of their hope and joy.

For the midnight Christmas Eucharist we were in the Anglican St George's Cathedral in Jerusalem. The service was disrupted by a bomb threat which turned out to be a hoax, but for safety's sake the whole congregation was ushered out into the courtyard where the service was completed, once again under a bright star-studded sky.

Such were the ups and downs of our Christmas celebrations in the Holy Land.

We met during our visit with a wide cross-section of religious leaders: Roman Catholic, Greek Orthodox, Armenian Orthodox, Melkite Catholic, Muslim. It was on one of these occasions that I was asked to explain the meaning of my cumbersome ecclesiastical title, 'Dean of the Province in the Church of the Province of Southern Africa'. I had to think quickly. Suddenly the clearest possible answer came to me; I was 'Number Two to Tutu'. This new and more colloquial title had two immediate advantages; it made sense to others, and it appealed to Desmond's sense of humour. From then on he took a special delight in describing my role in this way and receiving laughter in response. The phrase had its obvious amusing side, but for me it was more than a source of amusement. It became something to treasure as an expression of a complementary partnership and friendship in ministry.

Sadly, the Chief Rabbis in Jerusalem were unwilling to meet with us because of their perception of Desmond as a partisan sympathiser with the Palestinians. He did indeed sympathise with the Palestinians; after all, the bishop who had invited us to come was himself a Palestinian, as were the great majority of the members of his diocese. But

Desmond also made it clear that he supported the sovereignty of the state of Israel, morally questioned though this still was in some quarters. He also insisted on the legitimacy of the Palestinians' desire to have their own sovereign state in the Occupied Territories. We called for negotiations between authentic representatives on both sides of the conflict, with a view to making a lasting peace. This was exactly what we had been pressing for in our own

The two of us in a crowded street in Jerusalem, with Bishop Samir Kafity on the left

land.

We visited and prayed at the holy sites, particularly the Christian ones of course, but including the Western Wall, so sacred to Jewish devotees, and Yad Vashem, the memorial in grim and dramatic detail of the Holocaust. Desmond told reporters that he had found the visit to the memorial a shattering experience. He then added, very quietly I remember, that the Lord whom he served, himself a Jew, would probably want to ask: "What about forgiveness?" That remark was the last straw for conservative Jewish critics. Next day on the wall surrounding the St George's Cathedral precincts where we were staying, a strident and insulting graffiti appeared which proclaimed: "Tutu is a black Nazi pig!" Those of us in Desmond's group were enraged, while he was philosophical. To his credit the Israeli Minister of Religious Affairs, whom we met later that day, dissociated himself from the slogan and apologized for it. He did not take kindly, however, to the strong comparison we made between the injustices of our apartheid government and those of Israel towards Palestinian people.

The future chairperson of the South African Truth and Reconciliation Commission had spoken in a searching and profound way. He had done it carefully, without being dogmatic, in the form of a question about forgiveness. Coming from him it was legitimate because he had personally struggled with the same question in his own predicament as an oppressed person. He did not himself shun the costly way. Eventually he was to write an important book called *No Future Without Forgiveness*. It was essentially about his experience with the Truth and Reconciliation Commission. In this book he describes how in 1999 he returned by invitation to Israel somewhat fearful because of the negative reactions to him ten years earlier. He writes:

> "I need not have worried. Our hosts at the meeting in Jerusalem had to turn people away.... There really was a deep interest among Israelis in the process of the Truth and Reconciliation

Commission and in the concept of forgiveness
and reconciliation.... The process in which South
Africa had been engaged lent credibility to
whatever I might say that had previously been
absent.... More than anything else, it did seem as
if many who listened to me were people who
derived hope from what we had attempted to do in
South Africa." 2

By then Desmond was experiencing a similar reception
in his home country from many who had strongly opposed
him in earlier years. The 'Public Enemy Number One' so
far as the government and many white South Africans
were concerned, became, with Nelson Mandela, a revered
elder statesman and a hero of reconciliation. Many critics
had to eat their words and realize how prejudiced and
misled they had been.

Before leaving this account of our visit to the Holy Land
in 1989, I would like to add that its theological impact was,
for me, deep and lasting. Liberation theology, initiated
among the poor and oppressed in South America, had
struck a strong resonant chord in apartheid South Africa.
Setting great store by God's liberation of the Jews from
Egypt, it made the account of the Exodus a paradigm for
liberation from political bondages in our own time.
Desmond himself used this theme frequently in his
preaching, and it could not have been far from his mind
when he chose the word 'liberation' as the ideal and the
key refrain for his period as Archbishop. Using the ringing
words of St Paul, he would cry: "If God is for us, who can
be against us?"3 It was therefore a thunderbolt to discover
that, for Palestinian Christians, the Exodus story was, at
face value, not good news at all. For them it ominously
marks the start of a process which, through the
occupation of 'the Promised Land', led to the conquest and
destruction of their forebears. The Anglican priest, Naim
Ateek, whom we met and whose pioneering book called
*Justice and only Justice – a Palestinian Theology of
Liberation* was published in the year of our visit, found 'the
second exodus' when the Jewish exiles returned from

Babylon, a much more profitable theme because in that returning there was a more accepting attitude towards the other, indigenous people of the land. The prophet Ezekiel provided a better norm to follow than the tenets of the book of Joshua. "You shall allot it (the land) as an inheritance for yourselves and for the aliens who reside among you and have begotten children among you. They shall be to you as native-born children of Israel; with you they shall be allotted an inheritance among the tribes of Israel." [4]

It was easy to see how alienating and difficult for Palestinian Christians certain passages in the Old Testament were. It was hard for them to fit these passages into their contemporary aspirations as a people. Meanwhile, the very same passages could be given a strong nationalist interpretation by Jewish commentators. This is something with which we are familiar in South Africa, with the great trek of Dutch farmers into the interior in the 19th century finding its theological justification in the very story which is problematic for Palestinian Christians today, namely the forcible occupation of 'the Promised Land'. Where is the will of God to be found in all this, and what is the correct interpretation of Scripture?

The lesson we learnt afresh among our newfound Palestinian brothers and sisters was that the Bible is a complex book, easily misunderstood and all too readily misused. The Palestinians themselves had to be careful, with others, in this regard. The Scriptures need to be received not piecemeal, but in their entirety. Above all, as Ateek is eager to point out[5], they should be read in every part through the eyes of Christ who is for us their ultimate focus and their chief interpreter: Christ in whom there is neither Jew nor Greek, male nor female, slave nor free, Israeli nor Palestinian, black nor white.

We came away heartened, though seared, by our Christmas pilgrimage to the Holy Land. For all kinds of reasons, I knew that I would never be the same again. For one thing, a partnership between Desmond and myself, with much potential, had begun in the very place where the Christian faith was born.

Five – Endnotes

1   Editorial comment in *The Guardian*, United Kingdom, 21 May 2001.

2   Desmond Tutu: *No Future Without Forgiveness* (Rider, London et al, 1999), page 216.

3   See Romans 8: 31.

4   Ezekiel 47: 22.

5   N Ateek: *Justice and only Justice – a Palestinian Theology of Liberation* (Orbis Books, New York, 1989), pages 79-81.

Chapter Six

Political Violence at Home

"In my entire political career few things have (so) distressed me as to see our people killing one another as is now happening. As you know, the entire fabric of community life in some of the affected areas has been seriously disrupted, leaving behind a legacy of hatred and bitterness which may haunt us for years to come." (Nelson Mandela)[1]

One of the most painful complications in the South African political situation in the 1980s was the intense and violent conflict that broke out between organisations which were opposed to the apartheid government. In particular, this was true of Inkatha, which was later to become the Inkatha Freedom Party (IFP), and the United Democratic Front (UDF). Inkatha had been formed in the 1970s as a cultural and political movement, primarily in the so-called 'homeland' of KwaZulu but with an interest and a stake also in black politics nationally. In its earlier days it was seen by many members of the African National Congress (ANC) in exile as an internal front for the organisation. Inkatha's leader, Chief Mangosuthu Buthelezi, had in his youth been a member of the ANC Youth League. Buthelezi was also Chief Minister of KwaZulu and President of the Black Alliance, which was a loose collection of various black political organisations within South Africa that were opposed to the South African government.

A crisis point came in 1983 with the introduction by the government of its reformed Constitution, creating a tri-cameral legislature with separate houses for Coloured and Indian representatives, and still excluding the black African majority of the population from any representation in Parliament. Some organisations in the Black Alliance decided to participate in this new structure, while Buthelezi was understandably wholly opposed to it. Given these developments, the Black Alliance in effect began to fall apart and into the vacuum emerged the much more radical United Democratic Front. The UDF was a great cluster of various organisations, civic and political and including some church agencies, in opposition to the new Constitution as a travesty of true reform. Many of us as church leaders expressed the fear that the new tri-cameral structure was so flawed that it would unleash huge anger and new spasms of even violent resistance among some of the excluded majority of the population.

A referendum was to be held inviting the white electorate to indicate whether or not it accepted the amendments to the Constitution. There were those who thought that even a small step towards political reform should be accepted, whereas others felt that to vote at all in a 'whites only' referendum was distasteful and improper, as indeed it was. Others argued that the so-called reform was a clever device to co-opt two minority groups and entrench apartheid under a new guise, and that even though the vote was confined to white people, it should be strenuously opposed. I did an unusual thing myself at that time. While not presuming to tell other voters how to cast their vote, I gave public notice that I would be voting 'No' in the referendum. Whether this influenced the voting of others, either for or against, I had no way of judging. The revised Constitution was accepted in the referendum, and the disenfranchised majority of the South African public was left out in the cold.

It is in many ways ironic that serious conflict arose between the United Democratic Front and Inkatha, because both were strongly opposed to the new

Constitution of 1983. But Inkatha had opted to oppose apartheid through a qualified participation within its structures. The so-called 'homelands', each with their own limited government, were ethnic creatures of the policy of separate development, and KwaZulu was one of them. Though refusing to accept 'independence' because of the sham it was seen to be, KwaZulu was nonetheless intricately connected to this overall system. The United Democratic Front, on the other hand, represented the boycott politics of the period, which was increasingly opposed to all structures associated with the apartheid dream, not least what was perceived to be Inkatha's one-party state under an autocratic leader in KwaZulu. Moreover, the UDF was primarily an urban phenomenon, strongly supported by an alienated and militant constituency of black youth, whereas Inkatha's chief focus was rural, traditional and adult.

Meanwhile, as a result of the legalisation of trade unions in 1979, the Congress of South African Trade Unions (COSATU) had come into being in 1985 as a national focus for black worker interests. At an international level there was at the same time a resurgence of support for the ANC which, though still banned in South Africa, now received tacit support from the United Democratic Front and COSATU. Inkatha, in these new circumstances, was driven back on the defensive and became increasingly identified with its ethnic roots in KwaZulu. While Chief Buthelezi still sought to project himself as a national leader, he also identified himself with a strong regional option in the Province of Natal, seeking links with Natal business and agricultural interests and also with the Natal Provincial Administration. Would these combined interests be able to create an experiment in multi-racial initiative that would be an example for the rest of the country to follow? Or would they threaten to take the Province of Natal, with KwaZulu, into a political cul-de-sac?

What emerged in the ensuing conflict between Inkatha and the UDF in Natal was a struggle for political turf, indeed for the political soul of the people of this province.

It was not an inter-tribal conflict because the black members of both these organisations in Natal were mostly Zulu-speakers. The situation was complicated further by the role of the state, for the Nationalist government positioned itself in support of Inkatha against the more radical opposition. Buthelezi's firm disapproval of international economic sanctions against South Africa fitted perfectly with the government's position on this issue. The government's instinct, in spite of its disapproval of Buthelezi's decision to reject 'independence' for KwaZulu, was to put its political and security apparatus behind Inkatha. It soon became clear that the South African police and the KwaZulu police were acting in unison against the political designs and aspirations of the UDF.

The stage was set by the mid-1980s for the violence that was to ensue and to last well into the 1990s. How were church leaders to respond to these disconcerting and highly sensitive developments? The dilemma for them was that they found themselves on the receiving end of conflicting pressures. Co-option of churches, and especially church leaders, by political organisations is always a temptation because the church in South Africa is probably the broadest social reality that exists. It is not a political party, a trade union, an employers' organisation or a golf club; its membership comes from within all these sectional interests and more. Church leaders, as a result, are the recipients of many, often conflicting human signals. To this one needs to add the complication of their personal convictions, which must sometimes be suppressed in the interest of their constituency as a whole.

Yet, if church leaders are to lead, they need to be clear on political preferences. The CPSA consistently expressed its opposition to apartheid; this was a political statement, made on moral and theological grounds. When the debate moved into the arena of tactics and strategies, complications could arise. We have already seen this in regard to the question of economic sanctions, where in the end the church's leadership expressed a preference for specifically targeted sanctions. How was it to respond to the uncharted arena of serious, and even violent, conflict between parties opposed to the apartheid regime, especially when members of these political organisations were also, very often, members also of the same church? How was it to respond to the perceived partisanship of the state?

My own conviction as a church leader was that I could not and should not be attached to any political organisation or party. This was not because of indifference. In my earlier days I had been a member and even a local leader of the Liberal Party, which had given me my first experience of inter-racial collaboration around a common cause.[2] When I entered a theological college to be trained for the ordained ministry of the church, I resigned, as a matter of principle, my membership of the Liberal Party. It seemed to me that a priest must be free to minister to all in his flock regardless of his or their political or other preferences, and that therefore membership of a political organisation was not appropriate. This does not, of course, mean an absence of political conviction or concern. At its best, it creates a freedom to pronounce on political matters, precisely because there is no preferential party allegiance.

Other church leaders do not necessarily hold the same view. In our country's history we have had ministers of the Dutch Reformed Church holding cabinet posts, the most notable being the first apartheid Prime Minister, D F Malan. More recently, a Catholic priest, S'mangaliso Mkhatshwa, was an ANC member of the national cabinet, while the former Presiding Bishop of the Methodist Church, Stanley Mogoba, has been the leader of the Pan Africanist Congress (PAC). There are Anglican clergy who have been members of the ANC and of Inkatha, and in the 1980s there were those who joined the UDF. Desmond Tutu himself was one of the early patrons of the UDF (he resigned, significantly, when he became Bishop of Johannesburg), while the retired Bishop of Zululand, Alphaeus Zulu, became Speaker of the KwaZulu Legislative Assembly.

In February 1990, the very month when

President F W de Klerk lifted the ban on the ANC, the PAC and other banned organisations, the CPSA's Synod of Bishops decided that it was not appropriate for Anglican clergy to belong to a political organisation or party, let alone hold office in one. We stated that any who wished to belong would have to choose between this and their licence to function as clergy. This created a storm in some quarters. Why the inconsistency, some asked, between the past and the present? Why introduce this policy just when bans on certain key organisations had been lifted? My public comment was that, in the mounting political violence in Natal, it was pastorally essential for clergy to be able to minister to both sides, to care for people regardless of their political affiliation. The black clergy in the diocese had already come to this conclusion after two priests, one openly a leader in the UDF and the other an Inkatha supporter, had had to leave their parishes because their lives were in danger.

Desmond gave his rationale for the Synod of Bishops' decision in his diocesan newsletter. He wrote: "The Church must be involved politically. There can be no neutrality where there is injustice and oppression. But it can never be aligned with any one political party. An ordained person must be able to minister to all his/her people of all political persuasions. A PAC supporter would find it difficult to accept the ministrations of an ordained person who belonged to the ANC as one example. Political affiliations especially in the black community are a matter of life and death. How can a minister who supports Inkatha work in an ANC area?...Only a non-partisan Church can act as a mediator in the tense and volatile situation in the black community, where we still do not know how to accommodate different points of view. The Church must teach our people that you can differ in your views and still be friends. That is why we have said ordained persons must not belong to political parties."[3]

A new development was in the offing: the pull into mediation. This was a very challenging enterprise, and there was no alternative but to embark upon it.

Six – Endnotes

1 Letter from Nelson Mandela, in prison, to Mangosuthu Buthelezi, 3 February 1989.

2 The Liberal Party was formed in 1953 in outright opposition to the Nationalist government. It disbanded in 1968 when the government outlawed the existence of political parties with a non-racial membership. See Randolph Vigne: *Liberals Against Apartheid – a History of the Liberal Party of South Africa* (Macmillan, London, 1997).

3 *Good Hope*, newsletter of the diocese of Cape Town, August 1990.

The four bishops on their mission to Ulundi.
The other three (from left) are Sigisbert Ndwandwe,
Alfred Mkhize and Zambuhle Dlamini.
See Chapter Seven.

Chapter Seven

Early Lessons in Political Mediation

"Though now few eyes
can see beyond
this tragic time's
complexities,
dear God, ordain
such deeds be done,
such words be said,
that men will praise
Your image yet
when all these terrors
and hates are dead:

    Through rotting days,
    beaten, broken,
    some stayed pure;
    others learnt how
    to grin and endure;
    and here and there
    a heart stayed warm,
    a head grew clear."   (Guy Butler)[1]

Desmond presided over three sessions of the CPSA's Provincial Synod during his ten years as Archbishop. The first of these was in Durban in June 1989. My wife, Dorrie, and I had the pleasure of having him and his wife, Leah, to stay with us in our home for the duration of the Synod. As was to be expected, a resolution was passed at this particular Synod about the political violence that was engulfing the Province of Natal. The resolution went beyond an expression of pious hope for peace. Prompted by the urgency of the situation and also by the fact that Mangosuthu Buthelezi had sent a 'message of goodwill' to the Synod, the resolution asked for an Anglican delegation to be sent immediately to negotiate with the Chief Minister, himself an Anglican. Desmond consulted about the composition of the delegation with Simon Mtimkhulu who was a lay representative at the Synod and happened also to be Speaker of the KwaZulu Legislative Assembly. Mtimkhulu diplomatically suggested three bishops who, he felt, would be acceptable because they were Zulus: Bishops Zambuhle Dlamini, Alfred Mkhize and Sigisbert Ndwandwe. Desmond, always with an eye to inclusiveness, decided to widen the representation by asking me to be part of the group as well.

The Chief Minister agreed to meet with us and we left the Synod for Ulundi fortified by the prayers and solidarity of its members. This meeting was for me the first of several such meetings in Ulundi, the capital of KwaZulu, with Chief Minister Buthelezi and members of his cabinet. As we travelled the three-hour journey by car from Durban, I reflected on my only previous experience of a significant meeting with Mangosuthu Buthelezi. This was in September 1985 in the same house in Durban where Desmond and Leah were now staying with us during the Provincial Synod. It had been suggested by a small group of clergy in the diocese of Natal who were concerned about the breakdown in relations between Buthelezi and Tutu since the funeral in March 1978 for the Pan Africanist Congress (PAC) leader, Robert Sobukwe at Graaff Reinet. Buthelezi had come to attend the funeral because of his admiration for Sobukwe, and some of the young people in the crowd became restless and threatening when he arrived. Desmond, who was General Secretary of the South African Council of Churches, had been asked to preside over the service. He advised Chief Buthelezi that it would be in the interests of his personal safety for him to leave. Reluctantly, Buthelezi left, but as he did so he was injured in the leg by a thrown stone.[2] His chauffeur fired a warning shot in the air, which made the atmosphere even more tense. What had been intended as a helpful and humane gesture on Desmond's part unfortunately gathered political connotations, inflamed by Buthelezi's understandable sense of humiliation. A serious rift developed between the two men. Time passed until correspondence took place between them in 1984 after Desmond had suggested a meeting. This meeting proved difficult to arrange because of busy schedules and because Desmond was overseas on a sabbatical for the latter half of 1984. Within that period two highly significant things happened in his life and career. He was awarded the Nobel Peace Prize, and he was chosen by the Synod of Bishops to be Bishop of Johannesburg. A healing of the rift between Desmond and Chief Buthelezi seemed more important than ever.

This was the background to the meeting in my home in Durban in September 1985. Mangosuthu Buthelezi brought a group of colleagues and supporters with him, and the three Natal clergy who had asked initially for the meeting were also present. Desmond came alone from Johannesburg. It was a tense meeting, with Buthelezi reading a lengthy and blunt memorandum[3] to the group present. Desmond did his best to respond. He explained, for instance, that while Buthelezi clearly had strong leadership qualities, his involvement in 'homeland' politics prevented him from being seen by most black South Africans as an authentic leader. Precisely this had been the problem at the funeral in Graaff Reneit. Our discussion did not succeed in resolving the issues at stake, but we were fellow-Anglicans with a desire to find one another even in disagreement. We had worshipped, eaten and laughed together. The meeting, though tense, had certainly been worthwhile. On a personal level it provided for me, as the host and facilitator, one of my earliest insights into the intricacies of mediation and the mixed emotions it can raise.

The meeting in Ulundi four years later at the instigation of the Provincial Synod was memorable particularly because of its fruitfulness. The issue we had come to address with the Chief Minister was both simple and complex. Earlier that year, the leadership of the UDF and COSATU had, through Archbishop Denis Hurley, the renowned Roman Catholic Archbishop of Durban, requested a meeting with Inkatha with a view to having preparatory talks about peace. Chief Buthelezi accepted the request and invited them to meet with him at Ulundi. His choice of the KwaZulu capital as the venue was both natural and astute. The UDF and COSATU responded by suggesting Durban as a more neutral meeting place. Stalemate ensued. *The Natal Mercury* commented: "It was predictable that Inkatha's insistence that talks be held in the KwaZulu capital of Ulundi would be regarded by the UDF and COSATU as conferring, at the very least, an unacceptable psychological advantage.... Where strong passions are involved, such details are not easily resolved. It took eight months to agree just on the seating arrangements for the conference that eventually ended the fighting in Vietnam!" [4]

Our delegation helped to pave the way for a breakthrough in the impasse between opposing organisations. The composition of the delegation had proved to be helpful and effective. Bishop Dlamini had grown up with Mangosuthu Buthelezi and was a personal friend. Bishop Ndwandwe was linked to the royal lineage. There was a tangible camaraderie present, which eased any tension. This meant that when the political posturing was over, room was still left for the pastoral and personal appeal. Buthelezi agreed, with the support of his cabinet, to ask one or two of his colleagues to meet at any agreed venue with the UDF and COSATU for an initial, exploratory meeting. Added to this, he indicated his readiness for meetings thereafter to be at alternate venues, such as Ulundi and the COSATU headquarters. The four bishops left the meeting jubilant over this small but significant breakthrough, and we reported back to a much-relieved Synod in Durban.

Contact was immediately made with the Natal leaders of the UDF and COSATU, and their response was positive.

The office of the diocese of Natal was made available for the initial, exploratory meeting, and I well remember how we tried to put everyone at ease over a welcoming cup of tea! An awesome moment followed when the two sides invited me, as a local church leader and the host for the occasion, to preside over their first tentative discussion. The outcome of that discussion was an agreement to set up five-a-side talks as soon as possible in order to pursue, in a more formal way, an agenda for peace. Face-to-face contact had been made, hands shaken, smiles given and received. The ideological debate about venues seemed to melt away in the presence of these factors, with the result that it was easily agreed to hold the first meeting at the Royal Hotel in Durban.

Interestingly, this further meeting took place in what was described afterwards by the participants as 'the most constructive spirit,'[5] without the need for any mediator or facilitator. This was by the deliberate choice of the group. It is of the essence of mediation in conflict situations that it does not impose itself, but holds itself ever ready. Politicians can feel diminished by the presence of mediators; they normally prefer to manage on their own. In a memorandum which Mangosuthu Buthelezi sent with his delegation to these first five-a-side talks, he included the following remarks: "I told Archbishop Hurley and I have repeated it since, that black brother now needs to meet with black brother, and that we do not need white midwives – or any midwives – not involved in the violence that is taking place." [6] This blunt comment leaves open the question: what happens if the baby has difficulty in being born? That is exactly what subsequently proved to be the case.

The five-a-side talks reached a consensus remarkably quickly about a peace plan, beginning with a Presidents' Conference in London for the ANC, COSATU, Inkatha and the UDF, followed by a Peace Conference and joint public rallies at home base, together with a monitoring and reconstruction programme. Unfortunately this excellent plan, which church leaders continued to press for in the months and years that followed, was not put into effect.

The earlier controversy about venues was replaced with one about numbers of representatives to attend meetings. The Inkatha Central Committee became uncomfortable with the proposed ten delegates from each organisation for the Presidents' Conference, and recommended an equal number for Inkatha and for the other three organisations put together. This was, in fact, the basis on which the five-a-side talks operated, but the UDF and COSATU responded by insisting that they and the ANC were distinct organisations which needed to be separately represented. Inkatha then wanted its affiliated trade union, the United Workers' Union of South Africa (UWUSA), and a bizarre group called the Natal PAC in Exile to be represented on the same basis as all the others. It is easy to see why there was this jockeying process over numbers.

Meanwhile, at an inter-personal level a much more serious obstacle to progress with the implementation of the peace plan emerged. Unbeknown to the five-a-side group, Chief Buthelezi wrote a friendly letter to Oliver Tambo, the President of the ANC, to test the waters regarding a meeting between them. He had not forgotten a bitter meeting between the two of them in London in 1979, which had initiated the parting of the ways between their organisations. Tambo suffered a stroke only a few days after the letter was written, and could therefore not have been expected to reply to it himself. But, Buthelezi would ask, was there no deputy who could do the job? The absence of a reply, or even an acknowledgement, was seen as a slight and also as a sinister sign of a lack of integrity on the part of the ANC about the peace process. This unanswered letter became, in my view, the key factor in Inkatha's declaration of a moratorium on the peace process by the end of September 1989. "We are hitting snags at the leadership level," said one of the Inkatha five-a-side members to me in a telephone conversation at that time. I had deliberately kept in telephonic contact with both sides of the five-a-side talks throughout those months. They seemed to be genuinely committed to their epoch-making plan. Informal contacts between them were maintained in the waiting period, but in the end their plan was not implemented. We had to await fresh initiatives for peace in subsequent years.

The four Anglican bishops who had been to Ulundi in June 1989 retraced their steps there in November, seeking to reactivate the peace process. After a warm welcome from Mangosuthu Buthelezi, we were given a revealing insight into a fundamental suspicion on his part. It was his custom at such meetings to read us an address, copies of which were always made available. On this occasion he said: "In February this year Mr Oliver Tambo and Mr Alfred Nzo, amongst others, met with UDF/COSATU representatives to talk about peace initiatives....I have heard that that meeting conceived of a peace initiative, so-called, as part of on ongoing vendetta against me....Not one of you can say that, having received this information through my sources, I have no right to seek a personal discussion with Mr Tambo and ask him face-to-face what the score really is."[7] We were now dealing not with venues or with numbers, but with undisclosed sources of information about a meeting of which we were unaware. It became obvious that we had entered a political minefield with sensitivities and difficulties which made mediation work extremely taxing and quite unlikely to succeed. With a moratorium in place on a peace plan which had looked very promising when it was first produced, I reported to Archbishop Desmond that I was deeply disappointed that the plan had aborted. The midwives had failed to deliver the baby. Worst of all, the violence had escalated, beginning to spread ominously from urban centres into rural areas as well. As many as two thousand lives had been lost in two years, and worse losses were still to occur. We were told that Natal had become the fourth most violent area in the world at that time, alongside Lebanon, Sri Lanka and the Punjab.

Yet all was not lost. We managed to persuade the Chief Minister to allow two-a-side talks to take place in order to ensure continuing contact between the parties concerned. Oscar Dhlomo and Frank Mdlalose were the Inkatha delegates. COSATU and the UDF were represented by Alec Erwin and Diliza Mji respectively. This group continued to consult into early 1990, and I had the pleasure of being invited to join them for their meeting on 25 January, just a week before President F W de Klerk's epoch-making speech in Parliament on 2 February and the release of Nelson Mandela a few days later.

The initiative of 1989 had sown several important seeds, firstly by enabling some key political players to meet in a constructive way and begin a process of finding one another, and secondly by implementing, albeit in embryonic form, the vital principle of working towards a negotiated political future for the country. It is intriguing to reflect that from 1994 when the new democratic dispensation in South Africa began, Mangosuthu Buthelezi and Alec Ewin served in the same cabinet at national level, though continuing to belong to different political parties. Frank Mdlalose became the first Premier of KwaZulu-Natal and presided over a provincial cabinet that included both Inkatha Freedom Party and African National Congress members. Oscar Dhlomo for his part decided to quit the party political scene and set up an Institute for Multi-Party Democracy, which sought to foster a new spirit of tolerance, among other things, in South African political life. Could it be that the seeds planted in 1989 provided a stimulus for developments such as these?

But before any of this came to fruition, we faced in the early 1990s a continuing crisis of alarming proportions. A year earlier, on 3 February 1989, Nelson Mandela had written a remarkable letter to Mangosuthu Buthelezi from Victor Verster Prison. His first purpose was to thank Buthelezi for the telexed greetings he had sent for Mandela's seventieth birthday. He then went on to comment on the black political scene in Natal:

> "Obviously, my fervent hope is to see, in due course, the restoration of the cordial relations which existed between you and O. R. (i.e. Oliver Tambo), and between the two organisations in the seventies. The most challenging task facing the leadership today is that of national unity. At no

other time in our history has it become so crucial
for our people to speak with one voice, and to pull
(pool?) their efforts. Any act or statement, from
whatever source, which tends to create or worsen
divisions is, in the existing political situation, a
fatal error which ought to be avoided at all costs.

Far more information than I possess at the
moment is required before I can blame any of the
parties involved in the deplorable conflicts now
taking place in Natal. All the same, I consider it a
serious indictment against all of us that we are
still unable to combine forces to stop the
slaughter of so many innocent lives. The struggle
is our life and, even though the realisation of our
fondest dreams may not be at hand, we can
nevertheless make that struggle immensely
enriching or absolutely disastrous.

In my entire political career few things have
distressed me (so) as to see our people killing one
another as is now happening. As you know, the
entire fabric of community life in some of the
affected areas has been seriously disrupted,
leaving behind a legacy of hatred and bitterness
which may haunt us for years to come." [8]

This profound and far-sighted letter was addressed to
"Dear Shenge" and signed "Madiba". These were
Buthelezi's and Mandela's clan names respectively. Within
African culture it was a sign of special respect and
affection that they had been used. This was an important
and typical gesture from Nelson Mandela. Unfortunately,
as we have seen, cordial relations with 'O.R.' were not
restored. A peace plan was stillborn, and Mandela's worst
fears were about to be fulfilled.

Seven – Endnotes

1   Guy Butler: *Selected Poems* (AD Donker, Johannesburg, 1975), page 80 – *A Prayer for all my Countrymen.*

2   See Stuart Saunders: *Vice-Chancellor on a Tightrope – a Personal Account of Climactic Years in South Africa* (David Philip, Cape Town, 2000), pages 29-31.

3   *Memorandum for Presentation by Mangosuthu G Buthelezi, Chief Minister of KwaZulu, President of Inkatha and Chairman of the South African Black Alliance, at a Meeting at Bishop's House, Durban on 30 September 1985.*

4   Editorial in *The Natal Mercury*, 14 June 1989.

5   *Joint Press Release, Joint COSATU/UDF/Inkatha Meeting on Natal violence, 19 June 1989.*

6   Mangosuthu Buthelezi: *Memorandum for a Meeting between Representatives of Inkatha and COSATU and the United Democratic Front regarding Peace Initiatives, 19 June 1989*, page 7.

7   Mangosuthu G Buthelezi: *Memorandun for Discussion with the Rt Revd Michael Nuttall Bishop of Natal, the Rt Revd Alfred Mkhize Suffragan Bishop of Natal, The Rt Revd JZ Dlamini Suffragan Bishop of St John's and the Rt Revd S Ndwandwe Suffragan Bishop of Johannesburg, 13 November 1989*, page 2.

8   Nelson Mandela to Mangosuthu Buthelezi, 3 February 1989. Copies of this handwritten letter were given to the four Anglican bishops by Chief Buthelezi.

Chapter Eight

Mandela Walks Free

"About a quarter of a mile in front of the gate, the car slowed to a stop and Winnie and I got out and began to walk toward the prison gate." (Nelson Mandela)[1]

February 1990 was, for all of us in South Africa, a month to remember. For church leaders in Natal it was preceded by a meeting on 29 January with the Minister of Law and Order, Adriaan Vlok, in Cape Town. We presented him with a memorandum setting out our concerns about the widespread violence in Natal and, in particular, about the lack of impartiality on the part of the police. During that meeting Vlok was called out for a brief consultation with President de Klerk. He returned and told us, with a smile, that we would be pleasantly surprised by the President's speech to Parliament four days later. This was the only inkling we had of the famous speech of 2 February which opened the way to the fundamental political changes which were to overtake our country.

Nine days later, on 11 February, Nelson Mandela walked out of prison to continue the struggle for freedom in which he had been a participant and leader for over forty years. He and his wife, Winnie, spent their first night, at the request of the ANC, at Bishopscourt, the home of Desmond and Leah Tutu, after Mandela had addressed a huge rally on the Grand Parade in Cape Town.

I had the good fortune of seeing Nelson Mandela twice

in the month of his release, first at very close quarters and then from a distance. It so happened that our Synod of Bishops was scheduled to meet at the Ipelegeng Community Centre in Soweto later that month. I therefore took it upon myself in my new capacity as 'Number Two to Tutu' to say to Desmond: "You had Madiba to stay in your home on his first night out of prison. How about inviting him to come from his home in Soweto to meet us all in the Synod of Bishops?" Desmond took to the idea with alacrity and Mandela agreed to come. The joy as we received him and were introduced individually by Desmond was indescribable. The man who had been a political prisoner for twenty-seven years addressed us briefly in our Synod, recalling in particular his gratitude for visits from chaplains to the prisoners on Robben Island and for the services of worship that they had conducted. One of them even managed to smuggle in a copy of the *Sunday Times* for the prisoners to read! He paid tribute to the church for the stand it had taken against apartheid, and especially to Desmond for his courageous prophetic leadership as 'the archbishop of the people'. One of the tasks falling to the Dean of the Province was to express gratitude on the Synod's behalf to any visitor. It was not easy to find words, let alone the right ones, on this occasion, but I count it one of the special privileges of my ministry to have had the chance to say 'thank you' to Nelson Mandela within a mere fortnight of his release from prison.

The second time I saw him was at a vast rally at King's Park in Durban on 25 February. He spoke to a crowd estimated to number 100 000. This provided a different kind of excitement, but it also had its disturbing side. He revealed the deep and painful feelings about the violence which he had shown in his letter to Chief Buthelezi almost exactly a year earlier, by issuing his famous challenge: "Take your guns, your knives and your pangas,[2] and throw them into the sea!" It was at this point that quite a number of people in the crowd began to leave, and we knew that it would be a long time before his idealism would be translated into reality.

Was Nelson Mandela naïve about the political violence?

The joyful reception of Nelson Mandela by the Anglican bishops.

Desmond introducing Nelson Mandela individually to each bishop.

People would say: "How can he tell us to throw our guns and knives into the sea when we need them for self-defence? Does he not know what is happening here?" For Mandela there was a crucial moral difference between an armed struggle against an unjust tyranny, which he himself had embraced, and armed violence between political organizations which have the same essential goal, though their strategies may differ. He has recorded in his autobiography that one of the first people he telephoned after his release from prison was Mangosuthu Buthelezi.[3] He also wanted to meet with him as soon as possible. Buthelezi, in his turn, invited him to come to his home, "KwaPhindangene" at Mahlabathini. There was mutual respect between these two leaders at a personal level, but each was also caught in the web of the internecine politics and violence of that time. What seemed a natural and obvious friendly contact between the two political leaders became enormously difficult to achieve. This kind of impasse is a paradox when people are dying on both sides of a conflict and the need for peace is self-evident.

As church leaders we were informed that telephonic contact continued between Nelson Mandela and Mangosuthu Buthelezi, but a personal meeting or a joint rally eluded them throughout 1990. On 25 March what came to be known as 'The Seven Days War' erupted in the Edendale valley near Pietermaritzburg. In a concerted Inkatha-led attack on UDF-supporting districts, several hundred people died and many thousands were displaced from their homes. It was in the midst of this crisis that Mandela took another personal initiative and suggested to Chief Buthelezi that they jointly address a public rally. Buthelezi promptly agreed, but he aborted the opportunity by immediately proposing Taylor's Halt as the venue for the rally. The ANC leaders in Natal, led by Harry Gwala who was a hawk rather than a dove, were adamant that their leader should not go into this Inkatha stronghold. Mandela felt bound to withdraw. If greater care and patience had been shown about a mutual choice of venue, the outcome would perhaps have been different.

Church leaders became embroiled in these sensitive

matters, for we too were desperate for peace. Desmond came on a pastoral visit to Pietermaritzburg, so that we could take him to some of the scenes of destruction caused by the Seven Days War. We went to be with the refugees who were being accommodated in church halls. We visited an almost completely desolate KwaMnyandu with many burnt-out homes. Among these we found an elderly man who, though injured in the fighting, had refused to leave his ancestral home. It was a poignant moment to be able to pray with him and try to reassure him before we left.

Renewed mediation was on our minds as well as attempts at pastoral care. As we called for an immediate moratorium on the conflict, we asked also for a resurrection of the very constructive peace plan of 1989. On 2 April a group of national and Natal church leaders engaged in a long day's shuttle diplomacy, meeting with Mangosuthu Buthelezi and his colleagues in the morning at Ulundi and with Nelson Mandela and his colleagues late that afternoon in Pietermaritzburg. We were the go-betweens, but this was the closest we could get to drawing the two leaders and their respective organizations together. Chief Buthelezi declared his willingness to appear in a joint peace rally at any stadium in the Pietermaritzburg area, but this came too late; the moment had passed, and suspicions had deepened. It was not until January 1991 that the two leaders finally met, and once again, as with the five-a-side talks eighteen months earlier, the venue chosen was the Royal Hotel in Durban.

What is the role of the church in a situation of painful conflict such as this? It is at least threefold. Firstly, there is the obvious duty to care for the injured and bereaved, and for those displaced from their homes. There is an obligation to provide tangible relief, both material and spiritual. Secondly, there is a duty to discern and declare the truth about the violence as the church perceives it: to name the causes and to make this known without fear or favour. Thirdly, there is the need to promote dialogue between the parties and to offer mediation in the interests of peace and reconciliation. We were reasonably good at the first and third of these obligations, but we fell short regarding the second. The reason for falling short was a good one, even if it does not exonerate us. It was exceedingly difficult, if not impossible, to play the role of both mediator for peace and advocate for truth. The result was that, in the delicacy of our mediation work, church leaders tended to be listeners and persuaders rather than critics. There were many times when we were tempted to be critics – for example, of the collusion we perceived between Inkatha and the security forces at that time. There were also many times when, in pursuit of what we considered to be the larger aim, we refrained from speaking out about the actors in the violence. Some will say that the church failed in its public prophetic role. Others will say that the leadership was wise, at such a fraught time, to tread warily, to be pastoral rather than prophetic.[4]

The one exception to our rule was in our dealings with the national government, though there was, of course, a change in our attitude to the government after 2 February 1990. Desmond Tutu was among those who privately and publicly commended President F W de Klerk for his groundbreaking and indeed breathtaking decisions. Moreover, we found our meetings with the President more constructive than they had been in the past. For De Klerk's style was to listen first and then to speak, to reason rather than to harangue. We had an important meeting with him on 11 April 1990 in the aftermath of our efforts in Natal, taking the opportunity of presenting to him a full memorandum on the situation of social and political havoc in the province. We argued strongly for a judicial commission of enquiry and for certain areas to be declared disaster areas so that proper relief could be provided.

We went further, and this is where the role of critic came to the fore. We had come to the conclusion, on evidence that was before us, that neither the South African police nor the KwaZulu police had been impartial and effective in their handling of the conflict. We called for a reliable peacekeeping force in the province. We were aware that this critique included by implication Mangosuthu Buthelezi because he was not only the Chief Minister of

KwaZulu but also its Minister of Police. How could his police force be impartial in a conflict that included the very organisation, Inkatha, of which he was President? We did not know at that stage that there was also clandestine collusion between Inkatha and the South African government. On 25 March – the day the Seven Days War began – Inkatha had a public rally at King's Park in Durban. It was their response to the ANC's rally there, which Nelson Mandela had addressed, just a month earlier. It transpired later that the Inkatha rally had been secretly funded by the South African government. As a result this event and others surrounding it came to be known as Inkathagate.

At the press conference after our meeting with President de Klerk, when we made our demands public, Desmond commented: "It was a meeting that was carried out in a very good atmosphere....I have to say that the last time I was in Tuynhuys there was a lot of finger wagging. It's a totally different atmosphere now."[5] That was true, but there was also another side, as we were to discover later. Politicians can become statesmen, but statesmen do not cease to be politicians.

Eight – Endnotes

1   Nelson Mandela: *Long Walk to Freedom* (Macdonald Purnell, Randburg, 1994), page 552.

2   A sharp and heavy metal instrument used in the cutting of sugar cane.

3   Nelson Mandela: *Long Walk to Freedom* (Macdonald Purnell, Randburg, 1994), page 565.

4   For further discussion of these questions, see Michael Nuttall: *Peter Kerchhoff and the KwaZulu-Natal Church Leaders' Group* in Lou Levine (ed.): *Hope Beyond Apartheid – the Peter Kerchhoff Years of PACSA* (PACSA, Pietermaritzburg, 2002), pages 188-192. PACSA is the 'Pietermaritzburg Agency for Christian Social Awareness'.

5   *Transcript of News Conference*, Cape Town, 11 April 1990. President PW Botha's vigorous wagging of his finger at his opponents, both in public and in private, became a well-known feature of his presidency, symbolising his autocratic and petulant manner.

Chapter Nine

Salvation by Summits?

"To those who are dying in the violence, the important question is no longer who is to blame but how the killings can be stopped." (Oscar Dhlomo)[1] "I would have no hesitation in suggesting that the Church should gear itself to play a more prominent role in negotiations." (Oscar Dhlomo)[2]

The long-awaited meeting in Durban on 29 January 1991 between Nelson Mandela and Mangosuthu Buthelezi and their respective delegations produced a written agreement which, if it had been implemented, would have gone a long way towards ending the political violence between the two parties. Church leaders had no direct role in arranging or facilitating this meeting, but Diakonia – an ecumenical agency in Durban strongly committed to the pursuit of justice and peace – published the agreement in both Zulu and English, while the Natal Church Leaders' Group, representing a wide cross-section of mainline churches, gave it their wholehearted support. Unfortunately the noble aspirations of the accord were not put into effect, and the violence continued.

Meanwhile, Desmond Tutu had called together a summit of black political leaders in November 1990 at his home, Bishopscourt, in Cape Town. This was the fruit of one of those 'divine nudges' (as he called them) which had come to him in his prayers. The most remarkable thing about this meeting was the range of its representation. For the first time ever the leaders of the so-called 'homelands' and of the liberation movements sat down together to confer on their shared future in a united South Africa. Desmond's skill in putting them at their ease was a major contribution, as was the fact that the meeting took place in the hospitable atmosphere of his home. He had invited a small group of national church leaders to be present as well, and he included also an invitation to his 'Number Two'. It so happened that all the other church leaders present, like the political leaders, were black.

Three 'homeland' leaders declined the invitation. Another indicated at the last minute that he had double-booked and therefore sent an apology. Among those who declined was Chief Buthelezi, and thereby hangs a tale. As the date for the meeting drew near, he had still not responded to the invitation. Desmond decided to make a special appeal by writing another letter. He would have taken the letter to Ulundi personally, but he had engagements overseas to fulfil, so he asked me to undertake the trip on his behalf. I invited the Bishop of Zululand, Lawrence Zulu, to accompany me, and we were courteously received by the Chief Minister. I was deeply aware of the responsibility on my shoulders, made the more so by the discovery that Buthelezi had already composed a reply, which he showed us, in which he indicated that he would not be coming to the summit. We knew that the Inkatha Central Committee had advised him not to attend. All I could do was to urge him to reconsider his decision in the light of Desmond's second letter, which I had brought with me, and in the light of my own arguments. He agreed to reconsider, but two days later a slightly revised letter containing the same decision was delivered by his emissaries to my home in Pietermaritzburg.

The logical reasons for Mangosuthu Buthelezi's refusal to attend were not strong. He wrote: "I remain convinced that my going to Cape Town would only be symbolic and would not serve any real liberation cause."[3] The essential reasons for the decision were, I think, twofold. He was grateful to the Archbishop for the extra trouble he had taken in urging him to come, but Desmond had put himself at a disadvantage by announcing that any political leader who refused to come to the summit would be judged by 'the people' to be opposed to unity, peace and liberation. Even if this was true, it was a tactical error to say so and to expect someone as personally sensitive as Mangosuthu Buthelezi to accept the invitation easily. The other, probably more important, reason was that Buthelezi had not yet had his desired one-on-one meeting with Nelson Mandela, and he was not prepared to meet him for the first time in the company of others. Sensing this further reservation, I made the suggestion in our discussion that an arrangement could be made for the two of them to include a personal get-together during the day at Bishopscourt. I had visions of the two men strolling in the garden under the shadow of Table Mountain! It was not to be.

The Bishopscourt Summit passed, making its unquestionable contribution to the shaping of a new dispensation, by bringing together such an assortment of political leaders in our fractured society. But, sadly, it too did little to stem the tide of the political violence in Natal or elsewhere. A church-sponsored meeting between Nelson Mandela and Mangosuthu Buthelezi had to wait until June 1993. It came about as a result of a quite extraordinary set of circumstances, as we shall see later in this chapter.

In the meantime a pattern of 'highs' and 'lows' gripped the nation as it struggled towards a negotiated transition to a more just order. A National Peace Accord was signed on 14 September 1991 by a wide cross-section of political parties at a one-day summit in Johannesburg, jointly sponsored and presided over by an unusual and effective combination of business and church leaders. I sat in the chamber that day between a Hindu monk and a Muslim imam with a shared deep desire for the success of the meeting, each of us in silent prayer according to our tradition. It was Holy Cross Day in our church's calendar, a day to remember God's gift of a costly reconciliation to us all through Jesus Christ, who had said in his teaching: "I, when I am lifted up from the earth, will draw all people to myself".⁴ Desmond was one of those who led prayers for the entire gathering. He included a prayer which I had written for use in the diocese of Natal. It went as follows:

"Lord God,
renew your Church and begin with me,
heal our land,
tend our wounds,
make us one,
and use us in your service;
for Jesus Christ's sake. Amen."

The National Peace Conference was followed in December by the opening of CODESA (A Convention for a Democratic South Africa), which marked the beginning of serious multi-party negotiations for the political future of South Africa. With a peace process and a justice process in place, the year 1991 ended on a note of considerable hope and expectation.

Yet hope at that time in South Africa could not afford to be a naïve or facile hope. Many times during those years I was reminded of the words of the renowned Dutch Reformed missiologist David Bosch, who had said that a Christian is neither an optimist nor a pessimist, but instead a realist and a prisoner of hope: someone who is called to turn stumbling blocks into stepping stones.⁵ In June 1992 a Philippino priest, Edicio de la Torre, visited South Africa, and in speaking about the situation in his country used a phrase that struck a deep chord within me, given our experiences too. He spoke about the need for 'sober hope'. This was in the very month when the massacre of forty six people at Boipatong in the Transvaal (now Gauteng) had occurred, with invading men from the notorious nearby KwaMadala hostel for migrant workers wreaking havoc in a community whose name meant 'place of refuge': men who were aided and abetted by members of the security forces. At that time we did not know about those based at the farm called Vlakplaas near Johannesburg, and their sinister shadowy role within the security establishment, but we had nonetheless become convinced that a 'third force' was at work, stimulating the violence, causing mayhem in black communities, undermining political transformation.

Events at Boipatong in June 1992 prompted the ANC to pull out of the entire negotiation process with the government. CODESA had broken down in a stalemate in May, but collateral talks between the government and the ANC had continued. The right-wing Conservative Party had been making some significant gains in bye-elections, and President de Klerk, in a bold move, had gone to the white electorate in a referendum in March. He was given very clear support for the continuation of his reform programme. Now came the ANC's turn for its 'referendum'. In June it embarked on rolling mass action to prove its power among the voteless majority of the population. A further tragedy – the massacre at Bisho, when Ciskeian soldiers fired on protesting marchers, killing twenty-nine people – followed in September.[6]

Boipatong and Bisho caused emotions to run high, but they also brought the politicians to their senses. The changes introduced from February 1990 were not irreversible, and the government was now considering a return to a state of emergency. Thankfully, an alternative was preferred. By the end of September 1992 the government and the ANC had entered their 'Record of Understanding'. There are two ways of responding to a logjam. One is to use an explosive device, the other is gently but purposefully to raise the level of the water and allow the logs to flow again. The Record of Understanding was an exercise in raising the level of the water. It led directly to the renewal of multi-party talks and finally on 3 June 1993 to the fixing of the date for the first democratic elections: the magical 27 April 1994. The Inkatha Freedom Party, and Chief Buthelezi in particular, felt thoroughly excluded by the Record of Understanding, and although the IFP participated in the multi-party talks that followed, he withdrew his party when the date for elections was fixed because a new constitution had not first been finalized.

The atmosphere, therefore, in June 1993 was hardly conducive to a one-on-one meeting between Nelson Mandela and Mangosuthu Buthelezi. Desmond Tutu nevertheless remained convinced that such a meeting was necessary, all the more so because of current tensions. The violence in many communities also continued to persist. In March of that year he had flown to Natal from Cape Town to join other church leaders in a pastoral visit to yet another scene of shocking violence. Just outside Pietermaritzburg, among beautiful hills near Mboyi, a vehicle taking over twenty children to school had been ambushed and shot at by men in balaclavas. Six children were killed and seven wounded. At the site of the killing, on a steep winding road, Desmond had prayed an impromptu prayer that came deep from the heart:

"O God, we come to you... wondering what has happened to our people that anyone, for whatever reason, could mow down children in cold blood in this fashion...Please God, you have placed us in this land, a land which is so richly endowed with all your gifts, a land that is being soaked so much with blood....

God, we bring before you the families of those children who have been killed and those who have been injured. We ask you to give them the comfort of your Holy Spirit. We pray that we in a small way may be able to console and comfort when we meet some of them.

We pray also for those who have carried out this evil deed, for no matter how evil they are they remain your children...

We pray for those who have been injured and we offer to you these children who have died. May their sacrifice be a sacrifice that will ensure that freedom and peace will reign in this land..." [7]

Afterwards we visited the bereaved families, who belonged to the Inkatha Freedom Party, to try and bring solace to them in their grieving. As was usually the case in such situations, the bereaved were not in the mood for conversation, but in their shock and brokenness they welcomed our prayers and words of comfort and were

Church leaders depart after their visit to one of the bereaved families near Mboyi. Others, from left, are the Revd Frank Chikane, the Revd Dr Khoza Mgojo and the Revd Peter Kerchhoff.

clearly grateful that we had come. We ourselves were always moved and troubled after such visits.

No wonder Desmond continued to press for a summit. He was able to achieve it through a couple of shrewd and almost impish interventions. During the weekend of 5-6 June he was in Pietermaritzburg for two important events. The first was the consecration on the Saturday, in the Cathedral of the Holy Nativity, of Peter Harker as the new

Bishop of Zululand. The second was the unveiling on the Sunday of a notable statue of the Mahatma Gandhi. This was to mark the centenary of the event on the Pietermaritzburg railway station when Gandhi was ordered off a train on purely racial grounds and proceeded, in the coldness of the station's waiting room, to think up the underlying principles of Satyagraha. This was the philosophy of active and costly non-violence which he was to implement with such effect, first in South Africa against racial discrimination and then in India against British rule.

It so happened that Mangosuthu Buthelezi was to be present at the first of these events and Nelson Mandela at the second. Desmond was not going to allow these opportunities for contact with the two leaders to slip by. During the giving of 'the Peace' at the consecration service he went straight to Mangosuthu Buthelezi to greet him with the gift of peace, and having received the same greeting in return, asked him if he would come to a meeting with Nelson Mandela if he were able to broker it. Buthelezi replied in the affirmative. Next day Desmond took a similar bold initiative with Mandela. I remember the event well because he asked me to be part of it with him. After the impressive unveiling of the Gandhi statue, he deftly steered Mandela into a corner of the room at the City Hall where a buffet lunch was being served, told him of Buthelezi's agreement to meet and asked if he would agree as well. The answer was straightforward; he readily agreed.

These were two profound moments behind which lay the aspirations and hopes of many. Breakthroughs in a political impasse can sometimes come in the simplest and most unexpected ways, especially when they are accompanied by a warm human touch.

Desmond was poised at that time to go overseas to meet some commitments, and so it was arranged that, in consultation with Bishop Stanley Mogoba, the Presiding Bishop of the Methodist Church, I would take responsibility for finalizing the date and an agreed venue and any other details with the two political leaders. Such things, as we had discovered before, are never an easy exercise, and the best of intentions can sometimes come unstuck on apparently trivial details. In this instance, agreement on a date proved to be more difficult than that on a venue. I vividly remember being woken up late at night by a telephone call from Nelson Mandela ("Bishop Nuttall? Mandela here," he said in his strong voice). He was following up, at the end of a long day, a message I had left for him, seeking clarity about the date. He said that we must be patient about this, there was no need to be in a hurry, a lot of sensitivity was involved, and he was still working on the matter with his colleagues. At Ulundi, meanwhile, the pressure was on to finalise the date quickly. I realized later that, once again, the intervention of church-led mediation was problematic for some of the politicians, suggesting that they could not manage on their own. In a press release, Carl Niehaus of the ANC was at pains to state that the envisaged meeting between the two Presidents was mainly the result of five months of negotiation in seven-a-side talks with the IFP. "We have always said that if there is to be a meeting between Mr Mandela and Mr Buthelezi it has to be very thoroughly prepared. Our feeling is that an unproductive meeting would be worse than no meeting at all."8 These were important considerations, but they could also, perhaps unwittingly, become a stalling mechanism. Were not the spontaneous and precipitate interventions of a Desmond Tutu, while awkward for calculating men, also needed? Politicians also had to come to terms with the disarming and sometimes uncomfortable role of the prophet.

The meeting was finally arranged for 23 June at the Lutheran Conference Centre in Kempton Park. Both leaders brought small delegations with them. It was a difficult meeting, lasting nine hours, with some very frank exchanges. Some of the media concluded that it was a failure, because the deadlock over the election date in 1994 had not been broken. But this was not its chief purpose. Desmond felt that the coming together of these two leaders in earnest at that very difficult time was of huge symbolic importance in a society that was still gravely lacking in political tolerance. In their joint statement to the media they declared that "both the ANC and the IFP, like all other political parties who are helping to make a new South Africa, have a right to exist and must cooperate in the creation of the new society."[9] Quite as

Nelson Mandela checks a point with his colleagues at the media conference after the marathon meeting at Kempton Park. In the middle is Mangosuthu Buthelezi.

important as any formal statement, however, was the fact of their joint appearance at this media conference.

Once again Desmond had invited me to join him for this significant event, which he and Bishop Stanley Mogoba jointly chaired. It was a privilege to sit in on the discussions and to give Desmond some advice on the proceedings from time to time. For me, the most important thing we did that day was to arrange for the two leaders – each of whom we had come to know quite well by then – to have lunch on their own together, without the presence of political colleagues. What they talked about over lunch we shall probably never know; indeed, we have no right to know. My own sense is that that brief hour was probably of more value for peace and reconstruction in the land than the rest of the day put together. Who could have known then that one day, not too far off, when Nelson Mandela was President of the country, he would appoint Mangosuthu Buthelezi as Minister of Home Affairs in his cabinet and three times ask him to be acting President when he and the deputy President were abroad?

Such a development was by no means automatic, given the political rivalries and dangers that existed. One awkward factor was the role of the romantic visionary and author, Laurens van der Post, a South African of Afrikaner stock who lived in London where he had the ear of the British Prime Minister, Margaret Thatcher. He had become a strong admirer of Mangosuthu Buthelezi and had introduced him to Margaret Thatcher in August 1985.[10] Van der Post had little time for Nelson Mandela whom he described in 1986 as "twice a prisoner: both of the state, and of the bosses of his party in the world outside."[11] By the early 1990s he was urging Buthelezi to stand fast and not to "touch it (the coming democratic election) with a barge pole."[12] Instead, in December 1993, six months after our Mandela/Buthelezi summit, he was encouraging his friend to prepare "for the period in which you have to go alone and take what you can of Natal with you."[13] He had wealthy friends and supporters who were prepared to assist with funding. Van der Post was bitterly opposed to Buthelezi's eventual pragmatic decision, on the eve of the election in April 1994, to bring the Inkatha Freedom Party in as a participant.

Here was just one of the cross-currents, among many others, which were influencing South Africa's body politic during those years of transition. Awareness of it now makes the convening of the Buthelezi/Mandela summit in June 1993 even more vital. Through this and other painstaking initiatives, by politicians and others, the country came to a peaceful solution in the end.

It has to be acknowledged that it was only the coming of a full democratic dispensation which eventually enabled the political violence to come to an end. Not even grand summits could do the trick, though they certainly made a contribution. Even after the first democratic elections of 1994, with a government of national unity in which the ANC and the IFP shared responsibility, it still took time.[14] In 1996, with the first local government elections in the offing, the date for these elections in KwaZulu-Natal had to be postponed because of continuing violence or the threat of it. President Mandela took a fresh personal initiative and, significantly, requested church leaders to mount a new peace process, which came to be called 'Project Ukuthula'.[15] This initiative, together with the work of the Electoral Code of Conduct Commission (ECCO) and the increasing co-operation of the political parties themselves, helped to ensure violence-free and fair elections. In KwaZulu-Natal no party had an outright majority. This led to the formation of a coalition between the IFP and the ANC in a two-party provincial cabinet. This, together with a behind-the-scenes mechanism for inter-party discussion, made a major contribution to the final establishment of peace in the province. King Goodwill Zwelithini, the Zulu monarch, also played a part by insisting that he belonged to all the people and was above party politics.[16] Government administration functioned both in Pietermaritzburg, the old provincial capital, and in Ulundi, the capital of the former KwaZulu homeland, while Parliament sat alternately in both places. This was an inconvenient, perhaps temporary but carefully balanced arrangement that helped to replace some of the painful spectres of the past.[17] Political inclusiveness and compromise were symbolically reflected in the new hyphenated name for the province: KwaZulu-Natal.

Many acute problems still remained, but politically speaking the province, and the nation at large, had begun to come of age. Mediation efforts, whether in quiet seclusion or in the glare of much publicity, would become a distant, yet perhaps a hallowed, memory.

Nine – Endnotes

1 Oscar Dhlomo: *Intricacies of the Violence* in *The Natal Witness*, 2 August 1990.

2 Oscar Dhlomo: *Inkathagate – Implications for Negotiations and the Role of the Church in Negotiations*. A briefing, 14 August 1991.

3 Mangosuthu Buthelezi to Desmond Tutu, 26 November 1990.

4 John 12: 32.

5 David Bosch: *After PACLA – What?*, page 8 (An unpublished paper read at a Businessmen's Dinner in Johannesburg, 16 March 1977). PACLA was the Pan African Christian Leadership Assembly held in Nairobi in February 1977.

6 The Ciskei was one of the so-called 'independent' homelands, and Bisho was its capital. It is now part of the Province of the Eastern Cape.

7 Quoted in Desmond Tutu: *The Rainbow People of God* (edited by John Allen), (Doubleday, London et al, 1994), pages 242-243. John Allen, Desmond's media secretary, had quietly recorded this prayer on his dictaphone as it was uttered.

8 Report by Brendan Boyle of Reuters, Cape Town, 1993.

9 *Joint Press Statement issued by Inkosi Mangosuthu Buthelezi, President Inkatha Freedom Party and Dr Nelson Mandela, President African National Congress*, Lutheran Centre, Bonaero Park, 23 June 1993.

10 JDF Jones: *Storyteller – the Many Lives of Laurens van der Post* (John Murray, London, 2001), page 416.

11 Ibid, page 417.

12 Ibid, page 425.

13 Ibid, page 422.

14 The National Party also participated in the government of national unity until its withdrawal in 1996. The former president, FW de Klerk, was one of two deputy presidents. The other was Thabo Mbeki of the ANC. Nelson Mandela

was the first president of the new democratic South Africa. He was succeeded in 1999 by Thabo Mbeki.

15   The Zulu word 'ukuthula' means 'peace'.

16   See, for example, the *Address of His Majesty, King Goodwill Zwelithini Ka-Bhekuzulu to the Cabinet of the Provincial Parliament of KwaZulu-Natal, Nongoma, 1 March 1995.*

17   The provincial legislature decided in May 2002 that its sittings would take place exclusively in Pietermaritzburg.

Chapter Ten

Pastoral Presences in Places of Pain

"I have heard you calling in the night;
I will go, Lord,
If you lead me;
I will hold your people in my heart."
(Daniel Schutte)[1]

There is one occasion I can remember when, with the best of intentions, I gave Desmond the wrong advice. It was something I greatly regretted afterwards and it taught me an important lesson. The year was 1987, two years before I became Dean of the Province. Persistent heavy rains in Natal had led to terrible flooding, with lives lost and houses and bridges washed away. Desmond was in the midst of a personal retreat at the time, and when he was told the news he broke his silence and telephoned me to express his concern. "Shall I come?" he asked. Aware of his need for the retreat, I thanked him and replied that I thought it was not necessary. He sent a handsome financial gift to assist with relief work. Some years later a letter appeared in one of the Natal newspapers highly critical of Desmond and including the comment that he did not even take the trouble to visit the province at the time of the floods. I immediately wrote to the same newspaper to explain exactly what had happened and to take full responsibility for his absence.[2]

After that experience I never again advised Desmond

not to come to Natal, even when I knew that it might be inconvenient for him. On Christmas Day 1995 we experienced a freak thunderstorm in Pietermaritzburg which, like the rains in 1987, led to flash flooding with much destruction and even loss of life. Some houses, with families inside enjoying their Christmas celebration, were simply washed away. Desmond had that month begun his new role as Chair of the Truth and Reconciliation Commission, while continuing (until June 1996) to be Archbishop of Cape Town. Apart from these commitments, he deserved to be spending time with his family in the aftermath of Christmas and an intensely busy year. Yet he came on a pastoral visit to Pietermaritzburg to witness the scenes of destruction for himself and to join with us in visiting some of the afflicted and also the relief workers to encourage them. Once again he left a financial gift. We attended an emergency meeting of the City Council where, in an unconventional moment, the Mayor invited Desmond not only to speak but also to pray for the city in its need. It was a sacred moment, bringing fortitude in its wake.

Participation in pastoral presences with Desmond, especially among hurting people, was always enlightening. I soon came to realize that behind the words and actions of an authentic prophet lies the passionate caring of the pastor. Behind this, in its turn, we find the faithful work of the intercessor. It has been said that to pray for others is to live representatively. This vicarious activity heightens sensitivity to the needs of God's world. Desmond's wife, Leah, has said that his prayers for the world are like 'a Cook's tour' as he moves around the world, nation by nation, mentioning each one by name. Wide-ranging prayer is for him a daily offering, often in the very early hours of the morning, but never neglecting an opportunity, day or night, to move into this mode. His intercession book, stuffed with prayer reminders and requests, would never be far away, and very often in his busy life, if a quiet space arose he could be found with this little book open in his hand. The prophet, the pastor, the pray-er: these were an unshakeable threefold cord.

Two major pastoral visits in which I was closely involved

The bishops on an urgent visit to Phola Park in the Transvaal (Gauteng) after political violence had broken out. On Desmond's right is David Beetge, Bishop of the Highveld

with Desmond related to the intense political violence of the 1990s. Both were in the Vaal triangle, as it was called (now part of the province of Gauteng). The first visit was to Sebokeng in September 1990 and the second to Boipatong in June 1992. I had a hand in bringing about each of them.

I have explained earlier how February 1990 was for me an extraordinary month to remember, especially in regard to the release of, and first contacts with, Nelson Mandela. September 1990 fell, for different reasons, into the same category. It was a month, running normally at first, which became characterised by powerful and painful memories. The Synod of Bishops was meeting in Lesotho at the Mazenod Centre for one of its regular meetings.

Archbishop Desmond was with us to chair the proceedings. In fact, he never liked to miss a session of the Synod of Bishops because he always said that, among all the many meetings he was expected to attend, these were the ones he enjoyed most. Through the companionship of these meetings the bishops found reassurance and a renewal of strength to serve in volatile and sometimes dangerous situations. We always resided in one place, and the informal times were as valuable as the formal ones. There was much banter and laughter, often initiated by our effervescent Archbishop himself. There was also an element of retreat in our meetings, as we kept a rule of corporate silence at night and worshipped together in the early morning.

As Dean of the Province I did my best to help facilitate the planning of these synods so that they would take place smoothly and without the sort of hitches that would mar Desmond's enjoyment of them. His chairing of the sessions was adept and skilful, with an eye for the really important issues over which we needed to linger. He did not hesitate to express firm views himself, which could be intimidating for those who differed from him, but he always encouraged participation from others and had an intuitive knack for noticing if someone was disquieted or unhappy. On this particular occasion he was clearly glad to be back in the diocese where he had begun his ministry as a bishop in the 1970s. We included a relaxed and happy pastoral visit to King Moshoeshoe II and Queen Mamohato, who received us graciously.

One day during this particular Synod a group of clergy arrived unexpectedly. Fearful and tense, they had come to tell their bishop and the rest of us about the terrible killings that had just taken place in one of the hostels for migrant workers at Sebokeng. Communal violence had erupted because of this. There was rioting in the streets, the barricades were up, and the danger of a massive police reaction was acute. The clergy from Sebokeng and nearby felt helpless and distraught in the face of what was happening. What were we to do?

Desmond, on hearing the news in the midst of the

Blessing children at a Eucharist, with other bishops,
at Odibo in Namibia.

Synod, broke down and could not contain his grief. I felt it was right that I should follow him to his room where I found him kneeling and weeping. All I could do was to stay alongside, waiting. Why, oh why, this relentless loss of life? Where will it all lead? What is happening to our country? These, I knew, were the questions coursing through his mind and pulling strongly at his heart. They needed to be given time. As I lingered it became clear to me that Desmond could not be expected simply to continue with the agenda as laid down in the Synod. "Now we shall deal with the item on the work of the liturgical committee." No, he would need to be excused, for his instinct was always to be where the people were suffering, if this was humanly possible. Perhaps he and Peter Lee, the bishop of the diocese where Sebokeng is, should go together? But then another thought surfaced, which we spoke about through the tears. Why don't we all go to Sebokeng? So it was that this idea, absurd in its impracticality yet fertile in its potential for good, was shared with the other bishops, and immediately there was a consensus that we should go.

Leaving at four o'clock in the morning, we drove in a convoy of cars through the Lesotho border into South Africa and on through the long wide expanse of the Free State to the place of our concern on the other side of the Vaal River. Word had been sent ahead that some twenty-five bishops were coming. A light meal was provided on our arrival by a kind and hospitable priest and his wife. Never before or since, I imagine, had they had twenty-five episcopal gentlemen in their home! From there we travelled to St Michael's church in Sebokeng for prayers in solidarity with those who had gathered. We could sense the tense atmosphere in the township. We went into the streets, all of us in our purple cassocks. A great crowd of young people recognized Desmond immediately and ran towards him. He addressed them, pleading with them to keep calm and not to provoke police action against them, while at the same time identifying with them in their plight. I remember vividly how, as he was speaking to them, a huge casspir[3] appeared on the near horizon and came trundling ominously towards us. It was attracted by the crowd and was coming to investigate. We were very fearful that its occupants might open fire on this gathering of youngsters being addressed by 'the people's archbishop'. A group of us decided to form a human barrier – a purple barrier! – between the crowd and the casspir as it came towards us. This was a deliberate risk which paid off, and I shall never forget the small guns pointing out of the casspir as it cruised past, as well as the tight tense faces behind those guns which we could almost have touched because they were so close.

We went on to the hospital to visit those who had been injured in the attack on the hostel, after first going to the hostel itself and the scene of the attack, so that we could have contact and another prayer service with the people there. The injured in hospital told us a lurid story of a group of unknown attackers at three o'clock in the morning, some of whom were clearly seen to be white men, for though they had blackened their faces, they had omitted to blacken their hands and arms. Who were these white men attacking a black township hostel in the dead of night? Was this 'the third force' which had been talked about, those who were deliberately provoking violence among black people for their own ulterior motives? We were deeply disturbed by what we had been told.

So disturbed were we that Desmond decided immediately to seek an interview with the State President. We were given one in a matter of days. He invited me to accompany him as his 'Number Two', along with his media secretary, John Allen, and Bishop Peter Lee. Part of the heady nature of those days was the way we could get to high places in the affairs of state because of the famous archbishop who led our team. I have described earlier how a group of ecumenical church leaders had met with President de Klerk in the April of that year. Once again now, he listened to us carefully, but then, with the cleverness of the seasoned politician, he began to counter our arguments and water down our concerns. He said that he would ask his Minister of Law and Order, Adriaan Vlok, to investigate, and that we would in due course be invited by the Minister to come and hear the results.

The meeting ten days later with the Minister left us deeply dissatisfied and disturbed. He had a fairly large group of high-ranking security officers with him. During the discussion, which was essentially an attempt on their part to whitewash the whole incident in Sebokeng, one of the officers inadvertently referred to the transcript of our preceding meeting with the State President. "Do you mean to say," I asked the Minister sharply, "that our conversation with the President was tape-recorded without our knowledge?" "No, no," he replied, "what my colleague was referring to was simply notes on that discussion." It was clear from the facial expression of his colleague that this was untrue. John Allen expressed surprise afterwards that I had not assumed that our meeting with the President would be secretly recorded. So much for the naivety of bishops who did not make a habit of meeting with heads of government! I felt nonetheless that I had raised an important principle, and I subsequently wrote to the President about it. I received no acknowledgement or reply.

No satisfactory explanation had been given to us about the presence of white men in the group that deliberately attacked the hostel. The purpose of this random attack, we now believed, was to leave an impression on the hostel inhabitants that it was emanating from neighbouring township residents. This would encourage so-called 'black on black' violence between migrant hostel dwellers and the wider township community. "Where is Koevoet?" I asked the Minister during our meeting. "Oh, Koevoet," said Mr Vlok, "don't worry about them; we know where they are."[4] The special death squad battalion called 'Koevoet' had by then ceased its nefarious operations in the Namibian war, since that country had happily secured its independence in March 1990. We now know from the notorious trial of Eugene de Kock that he and other operatives in Koevoet had been brought to Vlakplaas[5] in the Transvaal to continue their death squad activities from there. Was this the explanation of the Sebokeng tragedy? If so, the government was turning a blind eye to a ruthless and sinister activity from within its own security establishment. It seemed that we were witnessing a machiavellian attempt to cause mayhem and disunity in black communities with a view to entrenching white minority power, even while there was talk of a negotiated political future for all South Africans.

Similar events in Boipatong almost two years later did not quieten these suspicions; they simply reinforced them. In Sebokeng in 1990 the attack was on a migrant workers' hostel. In June 1992, in Boipatong, the attack was from a hostel – the notorious KwaMadala hostel – into the homes of a nearby resident community. Both attacks took place in the dead of night. At Boipatong police vehicles were seen delivering some of the attackers, and instructions were given in Afrikaans. Forty-six people, including women and children, were the victims of a brutal and arbitrary orgy of slaughter.

Once again Desmond was distraught by the paralysing pain of this news. We talked together on the telephone. I remember him saying, almost helplessly: "What can be done?" My instinctive response was to say: "We can go there, can we not?" He agreed that we should go immediately. Once again we were accompanied by John Allen and Bishop Peter Lee. One of the things about these sorts of crisis decisions was that they inevitably cut across other existing important engagements in our diaries. I take a look at my diary for 19 June 1992, and I find that I squeezed this visit to Boipatong in between a funeral, an important birthday party and an annual general meeting of the Mothers' Union. Heaven alone knows what else had to be cancelled or postponed. I sometimes wonder how we coped with the varied pressures, both ecclesiastical and political, of those turbulent times. In some ways, to be sure, we did not cope. It was essential to believe in divine grace given for each task. Desmond did a very typical thing within hours of our visit to Boipatong. I had had to alert the diocese of Cape Town to the fact that one of our Natal clergy had had a serious car accident while on holiday in Hout Bay. Desmond went to visit him in Intensive Care, and the priest concerned has never forgotten it.

Two days after our visit to Boipatong, on a Sunday, I

A father shows Desmond his child whose head was injured and whose hand was severed in the attack in Boipatong.

spoke at a service in Durban for the commissioning of officers for the ecumenical agency, Diakonia. In doing so I shared the following sombre reflections:

"I was in Boipatong on Friday afternoon with other church leaders for a pastoral visit. People there are shattered by what took place last Wednesday night. 'Pray that it will not happen again tonight,' asked one of the bereaved women we visited. We have seen the angry reaction to the State President's attempt to visit the township yesterday, and we have heard his reaction with an implied threat of something like a state of emergency again. The fact is that the changes which have taken place since February 1990 are not irreversible. The people who made those changes are still in power (more confidently, in fact, since the referendum in March) and they are quite capable, if they so wish, of putting their new direction into reverse gear. I think we have reached a very critical stage, where we may have to gird ourselves all over again for particular stands for justice which we thought earlier were behind us."[6]

It had been difficult to know what to say, or how to pray, without sounding trite, in our pastoral visit to a traumatized Boipatong, which by a strange irony means 'a place of refuge'. Yet just being there in a ministry of presence seemed to bring solace to the bereaved and the fearful. Ten days later we returned for the mass funeral for those who had died. Prominent ANC politicians were present, and some very strong speeches were made. The mood was understandably tense and angry. Desmond had been invited to preach and he did so with his usual flamboyant flair. While identifying fully with the people's pain, he succeeded amazingly in bringing a perspective of hope into the vast crowd before him. Before long, he had us all waving our arms in the air chanting that, in spite of the worst that could be done, South Africa would be free, black and white together. It was a 'performance', but it had to be in such a volatile crowd if he was to make any impact at all. An elegant, polished sermon in the well-tried Anglican manner would have fallen on deaf ears. The combination of pastor and prophet in Desmond knew better.

I have one final memory of our attendance at this massive funeral. As the faithful John Allen drove us away towards the Johannesburg airport to return home, Desmond took out his Prayer Book and Bible and suggested that we pray the Office of Evening Prayer together. As he led us, we were able to make an offering to God of the day's sorrowful events and bring the perspective of eternity into our country's desperate state. This was a time for 'sober hope' and for keeping on keeping on. We were grateful that we had gone to Boipatong, not once but twice, as Desmond put it, 'to pour a little oil on your wounds'.

Ten – Endnotes

1   From *Here I am, Lord,* a hymn based on Isaiah 6: 1-8 by Daniel L Schutte, SJ.

2   Letters to the Editor, *The Natal Mercury,* 13 December 1989.

3   A large armoured vehicle used by the security forces.

4   'Koevoet' is an Afrikaans word meaning a crowbar.

5   This is an Afrikaans word, literally meaning 'flat farm'. It was a hidden-away rural holding owned by the state, not far from Johannesburg.

6   Diakonia Commissioning Service, St Aidan's church, Durban, 21 June 1992.

Chapter Eleven

Enlarging our Liberty

"For every woman who takes a step toward her own liberation, there is a man who finds the way to freedom has been made a little easier."
(Nancy Smith)[1]

In September 1990 the bishops were in Sebokeng with all the socio-political implications of the crisis there. Early in the next month, on 6 October, a completely different event occurred which, like so much else that was happening, had a major impact on my thinking and my life as a bishop in the church. The Reverend Mary Au from Hong Kong presided at the Eucharist in the chapel of St Mary's Diocesan School for Girls, Kloof, in the Diocese of Natal. She was the first woman priest ever to have done this within the life of the CPSA. Having given my authorisation, I felt it was important that I should also be present. The event occurred during a Provincial conference of the Anglican Women's Fellowship (AWF). I was due to give the Kay Barron Memorial Address at this conference on the same evening as the historic celebration of the Eucharist. I had often conducted confirmations and other services in St Mary's chapel. Now I was sitting in one of the pews, watching a unique drama unfold. For me personally and for the church, something of special significance was taking place. The breakthrough was a simple and profound one; as I watched and prayed, and eventually communicated, I came to the conclusion with a startling clarity that the head of the church, Jesus Christ himself, could not possibly be disapproving of what was taking place.

In my address to the conference later that evening, I included the following remarks: "Tonight, in this Eucharist which we have shared, a new and important ingredient has come into the debate in this Province about the ordination of women: the ingredient of *experience*, which needs to be weighed and included in the ongoing intellectual discussion, the ultimate outcome of which is not yet known. We thank God's servant from Hong Kong for her loving contribution to our journey. The Eastern Orthodox are right: an icon is more telling than words."[2] Mary Au had been invited to attend the conference by the AWF President, Pat Gorvalla. It was Pat who asked me whether Mary could be one of the celebrants of the Eucharist during their conference. The Synod of Bishops had by this time agreed that no bishop would be called into question if, with clear and substantial support in his diocese, he invited a visiting woman priest from elsewhere in the Anglican Communion to exercise her priestly ministry. But this was not a diocesan occasion; it was a provincial one which happened to be taking place in the diocese where I was the bishop. I decided that it would be sufficient to consult with the Cathedral Chapter (that is, the archdeacons and canons), who gave their support. In addition, I consulted with the AWF conference itself, because I knew that it included delegates from dioceses where there was strong opposition, from their bishops and others, to the ordination of women. The conference gave its wholehearted approval, and all agreed to come to the service even though some would find themselves unable to receive the sacrament. Mary Au herself was commendably tolerant of these solemn preliminaries. Her graciousness and humour eased the way for everyone. She was simply herself, and her celebration of the Eucharist in broken English left its mark on the spiritual life and pilgrimage of our church.

Archbishop Desmond had unfortunately not been able

to be present at this historic event, but he came into the afterglow of it as he joined the conference the next day. He expressed gratitude for what had happened, because the ordination of women as priests in the CPSA was one of his major hopes and desires. Indeed, it formed part of his understanding of liberation, which was the theme he set before himself for his tenure as Archbishop: liberation, in its varied features, for both church and nation. So it was that he said in his Charge (opening address) to Provincial Synod in August 1992: "I cannot have struggled against an injustice that penalises people for something they can do nothing about, their race, and then accept with equanimity the gross injustice of penalising others for something they can do nothing about, their gender."[3] Amidst all the other familiar arguments for and against the ordination of women, the argument based on justice was a peculiarly South African contribution, the fruit of a deeply discriminatory history. Desmond's pastoral heart was also at work when he considered this subject. He added, in this same Charge: " We will be a more vibrant, a more gentle, a more caring Church with women priests, for ordination is not to power or into an elite caste, but it is for service and sacrifice."[4] An exclusive practice, he thought, is in danger of falling into elitism or the pursuit of power in order to protect or entrench itself. An inclusive policy of ordaining women as well as men would diminish this danger and be more wholesome.

Three years previously, at the Provincial Synod in 1989, a proposal to allow women to be ordained as priests had failed to secure the required two-thirds majority by a very narrow margin of thirteen votes. I was closely involved in that debate because the vote was taken on an amendment that I proposed to the original proposal. The original motion called for straightforward acceptance of the ordination of women on theological grounds. My amendment, which was agreed to as a substitute by the proposer and seconder of the original motion, asked instead for an acceptance of 'the Lambeth principle'. The Lambeth Conferences are gatherings every ten years of all the bishops of the worldwide Anglican Communion under the presidency of the Archbishop of Canterbury. The Conference in 1978 made a decision to respect any Province in the Communion that wished to proceed with the ordination of women priests, while continuing to respect those Provinces which were unwilling to make this change. The Conference of 1988 passed an almost identical resolution in regard to women bishops. My proposal at the CPSA's Provincial Synod in1989 was that we should implement this typically Anglican compromise *within* a Province by allowing dioceses who wished to ordain women to do so and respecting those which did not. In commending this course I spoke as follows: "We recognise that there are deep arguments on both sides of this debate. We have to live in this creative tension. We should therefore avoid expressions of finality, certainly at this stage, and focus instead on what should be done rather than on what should be thought."

It seemed to me that it would be easier for those with reservations to accept such a decision than to vote on the theological issue itself. I described myself as cautiously open and suspected that there were others in the same position. Some thought that my 'Lambeth principle' amendment was a refusal to face the key issue and inappropriate within the framework of a Province. They may have been right, yet even if the original proposal had gone through, some bishops would in practice have proceeded to ordain women priests and some would not have done so, depending on their convictions on the matter. I was attempting to highlight that reality.

It was a painful and tortuous time because feelings ran deep on both sides of the debate. Desmond expressed his own hurt at the outcome of the 1989 decision, but then added something that was not easy for him to say. He said thoughtfully: "Maybe the Holy Spirit is saying 'Wait'." To be lifted into a stature of waiting, not in empty resignation but in the expectant biblical meaning of that word, provided a new perspective. His words turned out to be very perceptive, for three years later, when Provincial Synod again addressed the issue, the ordination of women as priests was accepted by a majority of just under 80%.

Four bishops had been responsible for making the proposal and the amendment in 1989. In 1992 a priest and a lay woman took the lead. In the intervening period, two important conferences had taken place, the first organised by women entirely for women, the second on the ordination question specifically and with delegates, for and against, from every diocese. I had the daunting task of chairing this second conference. Desmond wrote to me afterwards to say: " I am writing on behalf of the Province and on my own behalf to thank you most warmly....I think all the participants will bear me out when I say I think it was far, far better than we had any reason to expect... I hope that our Provincial Synod will as a consequence be the venue of informed debate without rancour and acrimony."[5]

Meanwhile, the Synod of Bishops, which had initiated and helped to finance both these conferences, also appointed its own episcopal committee on the ordination of women. I was asked, as Dean of the Province, to chair this committee, which deliberately included some members who were against and some who were in favour of women's ordination. The committee fulfilled a vitally important purpose in that it not only facilitated ongoing debate but also helped to create an atmosphere of mutual trust and appreciation within the episcopal leadership of the church. This committee reported at every session of the Synod of Bishops where Desmond as Archbishop went out of his way to encourage the same atmosphere of mutual acceptance.

I had often preached and taught on the biblical theme of waiting. "Those who wait for the Lord shall renew their strength; they shall mount up with wings like eagles, they shall run and not be weary, they shall walk and not faint."[6] "My soul waits in silence for God."[7] "Wait in the city until you are clothed with power from on high."[8] It is a fertile theme for our personal life as believers: the costly willingness to wait, either when we may be unsure or perplexed, or alternatively when we may be too sure of ourselves. We were witnessing this same principle at work in the corporate life of our church, which was after all facing a prospect that would alter a tradition of nearly two thousand years.

When the decision came in 1992 it was clear that the waiting period had been worthwhile. There was great joy for many – not least for Nancy Charton in her eighties, who became the first woman to be ordained priest – but it was not a triumphalist joy. The decision in Synod was received very quietly. Those who were pained by it were deliberately affirmed and reassured. First Desmond addressed the Synod with this thought in mind and then found himself emotionally unable to continue in the chair. This meant that the Dean of the Province had to take over the chair at an awkward and challenging moment! That night Desmond lay awake for a long time. Early next morning he asked me whether I would second a motion he wished to propose from the chair, in which he invited Synod to salute 'with deep appreciation and gratitude the theological integrity and the devotion to, and love for, our Lord as well as the dedication to Catholic truth, belief, tradition and spirituality of those in the CPSA who oppose the ordination of women to the priesthood; and assures them that there is a cherished place for them in His Church, which would be impoverished without them.'9 I readily agreed to his request. In later years some were critical of an apparent turn-about on the part of Desmond, who had spoken so forcefully the other way in his Charge at the opening of Synod. Once again the pastoral heart had come to the fore, tempering as well as shaping the ministry of the prophet. Affirmation of opponents was now uppermost in Desmond's mind, while at the same time he declared his joy for those women who would be able to find fulfilment in their priestly vocation. Was there some theological inconsistency in the process? While disagreeing passionately with their views, Desmond had never questioned the personal and theological integrity of those who opposed his own convictions. This is what he was at pains to convey in his eirenic resolution, and I felt glad to be associated with it. The truth is that, largely due to the nature and quality of his leadership, we held together as a church on this question, both before and after the landmark decision had been reached. The 'Lambeth principle' of mutual respect, which I had been at pains to commend in 1989, came into effective operation within our Province. What seemed like a contradiction was, in reality, a paradox of creative tension keeping the church united, even in disagreement. It was rewarding to have played a part in a process which was both delicate and profound. Desmond saw one of his great hopes and aspirations fulfilled in a remarkable way. The three-year breathing space had allowed further time for the issue to be talked and prayed over. Acrimony had been avoided, and victory was followed by magnanimity. "God, I think, is smart," quipped a delighted and grateful Archbishop when reflecting on this process afterwards.[10]

There was an equally remarkable, but less dramatic, sequel in 1995. The episcopal committee on the ordination of women now began to turn its mind to the question of women bishops, the very question that had deeply divided the Lambeth Conference of 1988. Would this require a completely separate enquiry, or was the consecration of women bishops a corollary to the decision to ordain women priests? We came to the conclusion, on logical and theological grounds, that it was the latter, for any priest in our church can be nominated for election to be a bishop. At the next Provincial Synod in 1995, a proposal was therefore put forward that the ordination of women to the episcopate be accepted as 'a logical consequence of the CPSA's decision to provide for the ordination of women to the priesthood'.[11] This proposal was accepted with very little debate, and those who were opposed to the ordination of women chose on the whole to abstain rather than vote against the proposal. This brought a simple, straightforward and natural conclusion to a lengthy period of intense debate, which had gripped our church at a time when we were fully stretched on the political front as well.

The pursuit of liberty could be one way of describing the history of the Anglican church in Southern Africa; it is like a vein of gold in the quartz, shining in different ways. *Constitutional liberty* was achieved as we established our independence in law and structure, while still remaining loyal to the standards of faith and doctrine inherited from the mother church in England. *Freedom of representation in synod*, black and white together, occurred at a time when in the secular sphere racial separation was the rule. To our shame, women were admitted as members of synod only as late as 1970, exactly a hundred years after the first Provincial Synod had been constituted. *Freedom of thought* was pioneered by John William Colenso, the first Bishop of Natal, with his controversial developments in biblical criticism that have become commonplace today. *Freedom of multiracial worship* was defended, as the bishops, led by Archbishop Geoffrey Clayton, refused in conscience to accept the so-called 'church clause' in 1957, which sought to make non-racial worship in urban areas subject to the permission of the Minister of Native Affairs. *Freedom from all forms of apartheid in society* was the aim as we participated in the struggle to rid our nation of this evil in the latter half of the twentieth century.

Of course, this is an idealistic picture, with much of the church's story blurring and marring its legitimate pursuit of liberty. Sometimes the gold was not visible in the quartz. But the vein was nonetheless there, and the decision to agree to the ordination of women can be seen as another sign of it. The pursuit of liberty within the church, and beyond it, was all of one piece. Unless everyone was free, no one was truly free.

Eleven – Endnotes

1 "For Every Woman", published in *Women Spirit Rising: Towards Wholeness*, a booklet distributed at the Lambeth Conference of Anglican Bishops, Canterbury, July-August 1988.

2 This address was published in Denise Ackermann, Jonathan A Draper and Emma Mashinini (eds.): *Women Hold Up Half the Sky* (Cluster Publications, Pietermaritzburg, 1991), pages 267-273.

3 *Charge to Provincial Synod by the Most Revd Desmond Tutu,* 11 August 1992, page 7.

4 Ibid, pages 7-8.

5 Letter to me, 3 April 1992.

6 Isaiah 40: 31.

7 Psalm 62: 1.

8 Luke 24: 49.

9 *Acts and Resolutions of the Twenty Seventh Session of the Provincial Synod, 1992,* 1992, page 100.

10 Stephen Coan: *Is Tutu Changed? Even He's Unsure* in *The Natal Witness*, 27 March 1995.

11 *Acts and Resolutions of the Twenty Eighth Session of the Provincial Synod, 1995,* 1995, page 76.

A formal moment in St George's Cathedral, Cape Town.

Chapter Twelve

Keeping the Clock Ticking

"Survival is only possible if there is a rigorous discipline in excluding things which do not matter and in limiting painfully the things that do." (Michael Ramsey)[1]

Before November 1989, when I was elected to be 'Number Two to Tutu', the role of Dean of the Province was on the whole a nominal one. One of his tasks was, and continued to be, that of proposing votes of thanks at the end of meetings or, as we have already seen, when we received prominent visitors to our gatherings. One major, but rare, function for the Dean of the Province was to take the chair at the election of an Archbishop of Cape Town. This came my way in 1996 at the time of Desmond's retirement.

Desmond decided to turn the role into a more substantial one, given the circumstances of his very wide-ranging ministry and his preference for delegation wherever possible. On 6 December 1989 I had unwittingly opened the door to this possibility by writing to him as follows:

"My dear Desmond,
Thank you for the warmth of your welcome to us in Cape Town and for your fine and caring leadership of our two meetings. I gather that you

have been to the United States since then; may
God keep you strong for your wide and exacting
ministry. I hope that, as Dean, I shall be able to
ease your load a little at home base. Thank you
for your welcome to me in this new capacity."

Any bishop, I imagine, finds it challenging to keep up
with the varied demands and expectations that come his
or her way. I remember reading with empathy and a strong
sense of identification the account of an interview with
Robert Runcie when he was Archbishop of Canterbury; of
how "occasions kept coming up at him: a visit from an
East German bishop, two sermons at Oxford, a lecture on
education and morality."[2] For Desmond life at
Bishopscourt, where he lived and worked, was also hectic,
both for himself and for all his staff. A shrewd compromise
had to be worked out for the many whom he could not
possibly see individually. Such people would be invited to
the morning tea break in the library. There they would
have the opportunity to shake the Archbishop's hand and,
if they were lucky, to have a few words with him. It was
enough. The room would be filled with laughter and eager
conversation. For visitors from overseas especially, this left
an indelible impression. After half an hour Desmond
would be gone, for a media interview, or to his desk, or for
a visit to a sick priest or to a township in turmoil or to the
State President. Visits abroad and to other parts of Africa
became as familiar to him as visits nearer home. He was
always 'on the road', and as a campaigner for justice and
peace the world was his parish.

One of the things Desmond did not delegate was the
writing of his sermons and speeches. They all have his
authentic and passionate touch. He would compose in all
kinds of different settings. I have seen him doing so during
a long drawn-out service as hundreds of people came
forward to receive the Holy Communion. Having preached
earlier in the service, he would now be preparing an
address for the next imminent occasion, perhaps across
the seas. Much drafting took place, I suspect, early in the
morning while it was still dark. One saving grace was that

he did not hesitate to repeat himself. He had a collection of sermons, and of stories and jokes, on which he would draw, tailoring each to suit the occasion. Like any good preacher he also pursued favourite themes, such as transfiguration, justice, forgiveness, the sheer goodness of God. As a good *African* preacher he would adapt and improvise and be spontaneous, as well as being well prepared. We invited him to preach at the 90th anniversary celebration of the Mothers' Union in Natal. He said afterwards that he had prepared a sermon which tackled the subject of male chauvinism, but in the atmosphere which unfolded, he felt drawn to preach instead about "the compassion and the gentleness of God, the woman-like qualities of God....My sermon affected me more than I suppose it affected other people."[3] When a preacher preaches to himself as well as to others, the effect on others is more likely to be profound.

I was not the only ecclesiastical partner who came alongside Desmond as this extraordinary ministry of prophet and pastor, both in his own country and on the world stage, played itself out. He had each of the other bishops to rely on also as part of an episcopal team. In the diocese of Cape Town he had the support of three suffragan bishops. His personal secretary, Lavinia Crawford-Browne, was invaluable, as were his series of chaplains and personal assistants. John Allen, his media secretary, was a powerful support, often travelling with him, even jogging to keep him company in the early mornings. We strongly advised Desmond not to travel alone because of the security risk; a jogging companion was also essential. Desmond himself treated these precautions lightly, but John Allen and I can remember several occasions when we acted like private bodyguards (unarmed and vulnerable!) at airports or in townships, to protect him either from hostile stares or from such exuberant support that he was in danger of being crushed. Those were heady days.

He had another Dean in Colin Jones. Colin was Dean of St George's Cathedral in Cape Town and Desmond appointed him as a permanent Vicar General, another

Number Two, in the diocese. He was a key partner. "My
time as 'Desmond's Dean'," he wrote in 1996, "was a roller-
coaster ride of great excitement, and not without some
stress."4   He remembered the great public occasions. "I
doubt if we shall ever again experience those scary, yet
heady days, when you could almost see the angels which
Archbishop Tutu guaranteed were surrounding us in the
cathedral. I lost count of the times we followed his elfin
figure out of the cathedral to march with, as one wit called
him, 'Marchbishop Toyi-toyi!' His only question each time
we set off was 'Have you brought a toothbrush?' And shall
we ever forget that moment in 1989 when we were led in
our tens of thousands through the city's streets by this
extraordinary man who could make us believe in ourselves
and in each other by his unfaltering belief in God."5   Then
there were the more intimate memories. "Mine are of him
in the early hours of the morning before the 7:15
Eucharist, a little figure dwarfed by the great throne which
is his seat of authority in the cathedral. He reminded me,
in these moments, of a battery being recharged and I
always felt that these were times which should never be
disturbed. There were occasions when, on our mutual day
off, he would invite Pat and me over for a meal or a
drink....During these evenings as we were flitted from one
topic to another, he would sometimes get up from his easy
chair and drink in hand, do a slow shuffle in stockinged
feet while humming to himself. And Pat and I would know
that his tears were not far off and that he was missing
Leah and his children and that 'the slings and arrows of
outrageous fortune' did hurt, because Desmond Tutu,
Archbishop, Nobel Laureate, hero or villain, was only a
man too."6

My job was to assist at the provincial level and, like
Colin Jones, to be available at the personal level also. In a
strange and loveable way Desmond gave the impression
that he needed us. I discovered that what was best was to
be present, yet unobtrusive. There was no point in asking
too many questions of someone who had so much else on
his mind. Personal messages of affirmation and support
were important. So too was regular reporting, verbal and

written, for, as Desmond well knew, delegation is not abdication. Initiative and accountability became companions in a sensitive operation. I also had the invaluable support of the Provincial Executive Officer in the person, first, of Njongonkulu Ndungane and then of Rowan Smith. We planned many a meeting or synod or elective assembly and sat on many commissions and committees.

Early on in my Deanship I received from Desmond another of his handwritten postcards, which read as follows:

> "My dear Michael
> Just a little note to thank you very much for all your support, wise counsel, and everything you do so splendidly as Dean. I am going to rely heavily on you and I do so with very great confidence...
> Much love and God's blessings
> +Desmond."

This letter was encouraging because administration sometimes receives a bad press within the church, as if it is a waste of time and has little or nothing to do with people. The truth is that no large organisation, including the church, can survive without it. A false dichotomy is sometimes set between maintenance and mission. It is true that maintenance is not an end in itself – it should be *for* mission – but mission without maintenance is like a soul without a body. Moreover, administration has at its best a strong pastoral component; it deals with many of the nuts and bolts of caring for the needs of people, including employees who in the case of the church are primarily the clergy.

With these thoughts in mind, as well as a desire to provide maximum support for a unique Archbishop, I embarked on my new background role right gladly. I shall not pretend that it was easy, for it meant fitting additional responsibilities into what was already a demanding ministry in both church and society. I found that a day off

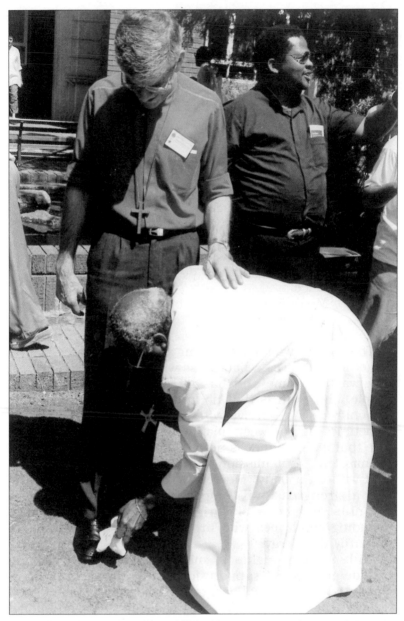

*An informal moment as Desmond uses his handkerchief to wipe
off some tea which I had foolishly spilt on my shoe.*

at home often included work at my desk. Wryly, we would add it to the Christian calendar as a "St Catch Up's Day"! When I became Dean of the Province, some of my work in the diocese of Natal suffered, in particular direct pastoral care of the clergy. Many were generous in making allowances for this. The truth was that we were living and working in tumultuous times in which normal priorities had to shift for a while. There was a price to pay, with success at one level often occurring at the cost of failure elsewhere. I was conscious of much failure, but I became aware also of a need to accept the larger view and to lean on the divine mercy.

The CPSA's theological colleges for the training of its clergy faced a crisis of identity in the 1990s. The ecumenical Federal Theological Seminary at Imbali, just outside Pietermaritzburg, made the difficult decision to close because of insufficient student numbers to keep it financially viable. This meant the closure of St Peter's College, which was its Anglican constituent part, bringing to a poignant and painful end the existence of a college, first at Rosettenville in Johannesburg, then at Alice in the Eastern Cape, and finally at Imbali, a college where Desmond had himself trained and taught. Meanwhile, the other two CPSA colleges, St Bede's at Umtata and St Paul's in Grahamstown, each with a strong tradition much valued by past students, were also struggling with inadequate numbers. The bishops came to the reluctant conclusion that it would be necessary to close these two colleges as well, and create out of all three former institutions a single new college which would be full and thoroughly viable. I was asked to preside as Dean of the Province over this very sensitive process, and I shall not easily forget a joint St Bede's and St Paul's meeting in East London where all the arts of diplomacy and discernment were required. Eventually the new College of the Transfiguration (drawing on Desmond's favourite theological word) came into being under the outstanding leadership of its first rector, Canon Luke Pato. The negotiator of the process was then asked by the Synod of Bishops to chair the new college council, and so it was that

I became closely involved with this new venture in theological education during its initial years.

The life of several CPSA departments was also in some disarray. Here, too, their cost was increasingly felt to be prohibitive, and as directors left or retired, they tended not to be replaced. The vacuums that arose were filled by already overworked bishops, who were now appointed as

This photograph was taken after the first Council meeting of the College of the Transfiguration in February 1993.
From left, back row: The Ven. Ezra Tisani, the Rt Revd Njongonkulu Ndungane, Prof. Peter Mtuze, the Revd Fred Hendricks, the Revd Wilma Jakobsen, Prof. Michael Whisson, the Rt Revd Peter Lee;
Front row: Mr Siyabulela Gidi (Student Representative), the Revd David Doveton (Staff Representative), the Rt Revd Michael Nuttall (Chair of Council), the Most Revd Desmond Tutu (The Metropolitan and Visitor), the Revd Canon Luke Lungile Pato (College Rector), the Rt Revd David Russell (Bishop of Grahamstown)

'liaison bishops' for this or that Provincial activity. This left an impression that our church was becoming more and more curial in its leadership and authority, which was contrary to the inherited pattern of bishops, clergy and laity taking responsibility together for the affairs of the church. Important priorities for mission and ministry in the CPSA had been set at a landmark Partners in Mission consultation in 1987. By the early 1990s these had begun to run their course. The socio-political climate had changed significantly; independence had come to Namibia, the war in Mozambique was over, South Africa was facing perilously but expectantly in a new direction. A new sense of focus and priority was required for the church. In fact, it could be said that we had come to lean too heavily on the example and stature of an exceptional Archbishop at the heart of our life as a Province. It was essentially his dynamism and character that held us together and provided a sense of purpose and mission. At one level it was natural that we should lean on Desmond. At another level it was a luxury that could lead to complacency. His leadership was not going to last forever.

In May 1994 another major consultation was held at the Modderpoort Conference Centre in the Free State. Modderpoort is in a beautiful setting, looking across wide plains to the Maluti Mountains in Lesotho in the distance. It was bitterly cold at the time of the consultation, with temperatures plummeting unusually to minus 6 degrees. However, our spirits were high because this was less than a month since South Africa's first democratic elections and the inauguration of the great and magnanimous Nelson Mandela as President, with F W de Klerk as one of his deputies. The justice and peace we had longed and striven for had arrived, and for the time being we were happy to enjoy the euphoria.

But what of the future? This clearly needed to be our consultation's agenda. Unfortunately, Desmond could not be with us, so once again it fell to the Dean of the Province to preside and, with others, to seek to guide the proceedings. We emerged three days later with three new focuses and priorities for the CPSA, which provided both inspiration and challenge. These were:

1. The healing, reconstruction and development of the nations of Southern Africa.
2. The renewal and empowerment of the local church.
3. An authentic and engaged spirituality.

Some thought that Focus Two should be Focus One, with ministry to society flowing from a renewed and empowered church. Others, among whom I included myself, applauded the setting of the first focus on our duty to care for God's world as the primary arena of mission. Some thought that spirituality should come first, while others saw it as the essential undergirding of the other two. This was a healthy debate in which no one could claim all righteousness. The three focuses were, after all, a trinity, a friendship, in which none was complete without the others.

Overarching these priorities we set some words of Desmond's, used in an address at the Federal Theological Seminary and engraved in a pavement feature at the Cathedral Centre in Pietermaritzburg:

"We are to labour with God to help God's children become ever more fully human, which is a glorious destiny."

Later that year, the executive arm of the CPSA's decision-making structures, the Provincial Standing Committee, created a new provincial body called the Commission for Mission and Ministry, and appointed a full-time officer to facilitate and encourage the implementation of our new vision throughout the CPSA. It was an important moment of re-organisation and re-direction for the life of the church at that critical transition time, and I was grateful to have been part of the process leading up to it. Out of it came a new impetus for transformation and change: a transformed church for a transformed society. My hope was that the vision would not become a cliché.

Twelve – Endnotes

1   Owen Chadwick: *Michael Ramsey* (Oxford University Press, 1990), page 120. This was Ramsey's answer, as Archbishop of Canterbury, to his own question as to how he found time for study, thought and teaching while also having the pastoral care of a diocese and a duty to take part in national affairs, not to mention other even wider responsibilities.

2   Graham Turner: *Robert Runcie* in *The Sunday Telegraph*, United Kingdom, 23 December 1984.

3   Stephen Coan: *Is Tutu Changed? Even He's Unsure* in *The Natal Witness*, 27 March 1995.

4   *Gateway*, magazine of St George's Cathedral, Cape Town, June 1996.

5   Ibid.

6   Ibid.

Chapter Thirteen

The Chapel of the Heart

"Someone mentioned to me that 'new fighters' in the struggle for liberation often are tense, harsh, and unfeeling, but that those who have been in the struggle for a long time are gentle, caring, and affectionate people who have been able to integrate the most personal with the most social." (Henri Nouwen)[1]

The Desmond Tutu I worked with and came to know quite intimately was increasingly an 'old fighter'. Given the gross injustice he was up against in apartheid society, he had good reason to be tense and harsh in his critique. He would say later that at times the provocation of it all had perhaps made him too hasty and passionate in some of his reactions. Yet if Desmond was incensed, it was always because of some major injustice against his people, such as the government's forcible removal of several million black South Africans from their ancestral homes simply to implement a policy of racial separation. It is remarkable that he could be gentle and affectionate at the same time. He was never so consumed with his prophetic calling that he lost the common touch or failed to be courteous. I would say that these very things increased as the years went by, so much so that there was no trace of bitterness or resentment in him, despite the pain, both personal and vicarious, that he had suffered.

One saving grace was his impish sense of humour which often broke the tension, not only for others but also,

I suspect, for himself. Here are a few examples, in all of which he jokes refreshingly and disarmingly about himself:

> "I suppose it's been one of those wonderful coincidences, if you like, that I am an African with a fairly easy name: Tutu. If I'd had a more outlandish name, it may have been more difficult to get our cause overseas so easily publicised. I think they've got this guy with a big nose and an easy name, and that helped to give people a picture of South Africa."

> "While preaching in Australia, I suggested to an audience of young people that they should applaud various people. I then asked them to celebrate who they were by clapping themselves. They gave a humdinger of a response. Then I said, 'What about giving God a standing ovation?' Well, they really did their stuff; they nearly took the roof off. Then, without thinking, I said 'Thank you'."

> "One advantage of my skin colour is that it doesn't show when I blush."

> "It would be distinctly odd if instead of saying 'I am thrilled to be here', I said 'I am tickled pink'."

> "Leah and I visited West Point Military Academy in the United States. At the end of the visit the cadets gave me one of their caps as a present. It did not fit me. Someone else would have said the cap was too small, but my wife said 'Your head is too big'."[2]

A second saving grace was Desmond's deep commitment to 'ubuntu', which is an elusive quality in African culture, not easy to define. He explains it as follows: "It is the essence of being human. It speaks of the fact that my humanity is caught up and is inextricably bound up with yours. I am human because I belong....A person with 'ubuntu' is welcoming, hospitable, warm and generous, willing to share....It gives people resilience, enabling them to survive and emerge still human despite all efforts to dehumanise them."[3] This was a fundamental guiding motif for Desmond's relationships with other people. It was a quality that sustained him, and many others, through dark days of racial oppression.

Equally important was the constancy of his prayer. At the centre and core of life and work at Bishopscourt was the chapel where the regular round of worship – Morning and Evening Prayer and the Eucharist – was offered on a daily basis. The Eucharist for Desmond was foundational, whether he was at home or on his travels. I remember how, on our journey to the Holy Land for Christmas 1989, we stopped over at Frankfurt airport for several hours after a night flight from Johannesburg. Very soon we were searching for bread and wine so that the Eucharist could be celebrated right there in the waiting area of the airport before we journeyed on to Tel Aviv.

In addition to formal prayer and sacrament, there was the personal dimension. Only rarely would Desmond speak about this, as he did in an interview just before Christmas 1990, about the significance for him of the chapel, his favourite room, at Bishopscourt. He commented:

"This chapel reminds us of the centrality of what we are about. We're all very busy with summits and meetings and so on, and sometimes we may forget our 'raison d'être': that we exist for the glorifying of God and trying to deepen our personal relationship with God."[4]

Leaning on this more general comment, he allowed himself to become more specific, diffidently risking some revelations about significant times that he had spent in this chapel. Still he uses the first person plural in the main, because both his spiritual training and his culture encouraged him to avoid as much as possible any reference to 'I' or 'me'. He prefers to be corporate in his thinking and speaking, but he cannot ultimately hide the truth that what he is talking about is very deeply personal.

"I sometimes get called, when there is a flare-up somewhere, then we'd come in here to pray. We pray when we hear rough news and we say 'thank you' when we hear good news. The September 7 (1989) elections when people were shot, was very, very difficult to take and we broke down. We came in here....when you didn't need to use words....or try to be holy and....well, we cried, ja."[5]

"Sometimes when we are very tired, we just sit down here and let it all flow over us."[6]

These glimpses tell us about two chapels, an outward and an inward: the sacred space which was the chapel at Bishopscourt, and the chapel of the heart[7] that accompanied him wherever he went.

Desmond wondered at one stage whether he and I would see eye to eye spiritually. For I had become involved in the 1970s in the charismatic renewal, which brought to many people a more lively sense of God's presence, often triggered by a vivid experience of the Holy Spirit. The Trinity of Father, Son and Holy Spirit came alive in prayer and worship. No longer a mere liturgical formula or an intellectual riddle, the Three-in-One became an intimate and homely reality. My initiation into this awareness remains a treasured memory. It happened one morning in April 1972 in a very Anglican way! I was reading and praying, on my own, the daily Office of Morning Prayer. I reached the canticle called 'Benedictus' or 'The Song of Zechariah',[8] and while reciting it, came to the well-known words of the doting father to his infant son who was later to become John the Baptist: "Thou, child, shalt be called the prophet of the most high...." The word 'child' lit up in a way I had not known before, and this gave me reason to pause. As I did so, a gentle surge of grateful praise began to flow from my lips in a 'language' beyond my own, quietly but strongly, like the welling up of a spring of clear water. This was prayer 'in tongues', which I came to understand afterwards as an 'oohing' and an 'aahing', as if before a beautiful sunset or a profound piece of art or music, when ordinary speech is somehow inadequate to give expression to one's appreciation. I was a lecturer in church history at the time at Rhodes University in Grahamstown, wrestling constantly with many questions, both historical and theological, earnestly serving God and others with my adult mind. This new experience was, I sensed, God's way of reminding me that in essence I was still a 'child' with a capacity and a need to be childlike in the divine presence. I remember saying out loud, as I prayed in the new way, 'This is ridiculous!' Yet I continued praying. It was a salutary experience of mystery and wonder. Having been ordained priest on one of the festivals of John the Baptist (29 August, ominously the feast of his beheading!), the use of the child, John, and his father was a divine stroke of genius that did not escape me.

The importance of experience has been acknowledged in recent Anglican thinking to the extent of being put alongside the well-known threesome of Scripture, reason and tradition. "The characteristic Anglican way of living with a constant dynamic interplay of Scripture, tradition and reason means that the mind of God has constantly to be discerned afresh, not only in every age, but in each and every context....Sometimes the lived experience of a particular community enables Christian truth to be perceived afresh for the whole community."9 I have already shown in an earlier chapter how a particular experience of a woman priest presiding at a celebration of the Eucharist became a vital element in my own pilgrimage of change on the question of the ordination of women. Of course, experience alone can be a subjective, and therefore inadequate, measure of the truth. Tempered by the other three pillars of Scripture, tradition and reason, it nonetheless has an important role to play. Moreover, it refers not only to direct personal experiences such as those I have described, but also to the importance of 'context' in the formation of theology. Theology does not exist in a vacuum, nor is it handed down unchanging from one generation to another. It is shaped by the experience of historical, cultural and socio-political contexts. To take one example, liberation theology arises from reflection on the lived reality of the poor and the oppressed, whoever or wherever they may be. Charismatic theology and contextual theology, alongside their many differences, have this in common; they both give a significant role to human experience in their formulation. The difference lies in the *kind* of experience they consider important.

Desmond's particular difficulty with charismatic renewal, as it swiftly became a new movement in the CPSA and elsewhere, was that it tended to minimise or even ignore the socio-political witness of the church. It could become an escape, especially for white South African Christians, into a cocoon of safe religious piety. Research subsequently showed that this was indeed the case.[10] At its best the movement, rather than ignoring the socio-political domain, took the view that any worthwhile change in society had to be preceded by personal spiritual change in the individual. Thus Bill Burnett, one of Desmond's predecessors as Archbishop of Cape Town and a prominent leader in the charismatic movement, wrote: "To try to renew society with unrenewed Christians is like a non-swimmer trying to rescue a drowning man."[11] The logic of this may seem sound, but in practice many Christians claiming to be 'renewed' became more prone to maintaining the 'status quo' in society than to challenging and changing it. Personal change was everything. Structural change, other than perhaps in the church where some sharp criticism began to be felt, was not high on their agenda.

Shortly before his election as Archbishop in April 1986, Desmond, knowing that we were both candidates, generously told me that he would be ready to serve under me if I were elected, though he had a reservation. He was saddened that my involvement in the charismatic movement seemed to have introduced a hesitancy on my part about the socio-political implications of the gospel in a deeply unjust South African society. It was a comment I needed to weigh and consider, even if I thought it was not wholly true. Meanwhile, in Natal where I worked, the crisis of political violence was about to erupt. My earlier preference to be seen as pastor rather than prophet posed an impossible dichotomy. Increasingly I was drawn into

the work of the Natal Church Leaders' Group as we sought
to reach out both prophetically and pastorally into the
oppression and mounting violence of our society.

At the same time an element of intolerance seemed to
have overtaken the minds of some in the leadership of the
charismatic movement. I found this disillusioning and
unacceptable. For Bill Burnett liberation theology was an
anathema. In an article in November 1986 in *Ichthus*, the
journal of Support Ministries which he had founded after
his retirement as Archbishop in 1981, he warned against
this "cuckoo in the ecclesiastical nest". He was referring
through this strong image to a brand of theology rather
than to a person, but it was hardly a coincidence that, just
three months earlier, when he was enthroned as
Archbishop, Desmond Tutu had taken 'liberation' as the
theme word for his period of office as Archbishop. An
implied reference to him was plain, as Bill Burnett
acknowledged later in his autobiography. "This meant that
I disagreed with the leadership of the CPSA. There were
some in the hierarchy who considered this to be disloyal
and Support Ministries was in consequence fractured.
There is however only one Gospel, and that is not the false
and pseudo-gospel of liberation."[12] I was one of those in
'the hierarchy' who thought that this critique was
unjustified in itself and ill-judged in its timing. In
consequence I felt it necessary to resign as a trustee of
Support Ministries. This was a painful episode for me
because I had a high regard and affection for both men. Yet
it became clear to me that support for the church in its
variety of emphasis and conviction was more important
than loyalty to a movement within it, and loyalty to one's
perception of the truth was the most important of all. I
realised afresh that my preferred theological position was
essentially catholic, as indeed, I think, was Desmond's.
Truth is to be found in many places, both within the
church and beyond it. We needed this larger vision from
the firm base of our Trinitarian faith and our awareness of
the generosity of God.

In August 1994 I found myself unexpectedly and at
short notice asked to be the guest speaker at the annual

Speech Day and Prize Giving at Michaelhouse, one of Natal's several diocesan schools. Desmond was supposed to be the speaker, but Bill Burnett had just died and his funeral service was to be on that very day in Grahamstown's cathedral. Desmond correctly and generously considered it important that he should be present at the funeral. I took the opportunity in my speech at Michaelhouse to compare these two remarkable South Africans, each from humble beginnings, who in God's timing became Archbishop of Cape Town. I included the following remarks:

> "Both men had become, in their different ways, somewhat uncomfortable to have around. They were challenging our complacency, in church and state. One was a prophet to the church, challenging us eagerly to receive into our life all the resources available from a living God. The other was a prophet to society, summoning us to embrace justice and peace, speaking out and acting against injustice in the form of racial discrimination and oppression....
>
> I stand amazed and awed by the wonder and mystery of our humanity, in all its beauty and vulnerability, its range and diversity. Here we have these two men whom we have been thinking about today....Could I suggest that, somewhere near the heart of the educational enterprise at Michaelhouse, there should be this contemplation of character, giving thanks for the tapestry of a Bill Burnett and a Desmond Tutu and others we can think of who inspire us."

I remember an occasion when Desmond addressed a clergy school, at my invitation, in the diocese of Natal. In the course of his address he referred to all human beings as 'the children of God'. One of the clergy present objected that the Bible made it clear that this phrase was confined to Christian believers, quoting the words in the prologue to John's Gospel: "To all who received him, who believed in

his name, he gave power to become children of God."[13]
Desmond responded immediately and passionately with a
reference to the opening chapter of the Bible where it says
that all humankind, male and female, is made in the image
and likeness of God.[14] If that is so, then surely it is
permissible to describe them as God's children? Here was
a difference of emphasis between a theology of creation
and a theology of redemption. Desmond was very strong on
the former, and there were some who thought that he was
not strong enough on the latter. Certainly for him the
human family was as important as the Christian family,
and the loving God was at the centre of each. The truth is
that both theological emphases are important and the
affirming phrase 'children of God' belongs, with different
nuances, to each. The children of the old creation become,
in Christ, the children of the new. God, the creator and
redeemer, embraces both.

By the time I was elected to be Dean of the Province in
November 1989, I was ready, despite Desmond's initial
reservations, for what I felt to be a wiser and more
balanced phase in the fulfilment of my vocation. This did
not mean that I had all the answers; on the contrary, a
new openness and searching had begun. Paradoxically,
this brought a greater sense of security, yet of a different
kind. It was the security of faith rather than of certainty:
faith not in oneself but in the faithfulness of God, even in
the darkest and most difficult of times, whether personal
or political: faith that even in the midst of judgement we
are 'under the mercy'[15] and that, despite much evidence to
the contrary, 'all manner of things shall be well'.[16]

Interestingly, Desmond was in the end more
charismatic than his Number Two, but not in any partisan
meaning of that word. In temperament he was more open
to outward gesture than I was, whether it was in Anglo-
Catholic ceremonial or in inviting a vast crowd to wave
their arms in the air, calling out after him: "We are the
rainbow people of God, we are the rainbow people of God!"
He learned to sing with delight some of the charismatic
songs that captured the spirit of the times and whose
tunes and words fired his imagination. Then, in 1994, he

came into a fresh and profound experience of God in his bedroom at Bishopscourt, describing this event afterwards to his Diocesan Council as follows: "I was overwhelmed by the realisation that God loved me, and I wept like a baby, not tears of sorrow, and Leah had to dandle me in the way you do a baby."[17] The image of the little child was once again evident. Included too was the familiar 'divine pressure' which had been experienced before. "God was saying: 'I want you to tell the people of this land that I love them, that each one of them is precious to me, that they are made by love, for love, to love, and that there is not enough time left over to hate, to nurse grudges."[18] A nuance of the feminine was also present. "I want to tell you that God is like a mother – God loves you, loves me, every bit of me, not just the good bit...You are precious....You are held gently in the hollow of God's hand."[19] Here were echoes of passages in Isaiah, chapters 43 and 49, long meditated upon and absorbed, now finding personal expression through tears of joy and as a gift not only for himself but for others as well.

One of the remarkable things about the CPSA during the tumultuous apartheid years was that we committed ourselves to the production of a new Prayer Book. It would have been easy for the urgency of the times to dictate otherwise. Instead, our church participated in a worldwide liturgical renewal that also influenced many other churches in the Anglican Communion and beyond it, not least the Roman Catholic Church after the Second Vatican Council (1962-1965). It was my privilege to preside over the Liturgical Committee of the CPSA in the 1980s, which were the culminating period of this important work. The task was a time-consuming and meticulous one, carried out by a dedicated team. Everything we produced was vetted and finally approved by the Synod of Bishops, where Desmond gave his unstinting support and encouragement. Finally, during the Provincial Synod of 1989, which was significant (as we have seen) for several other events and initiatives, the new Prayer Book was launched not only in its English version but also in four of the other languages used in the Province.[20] Further translations followed later.

Just at the time when we were facing critical issues of socio-political transition in Southern Africa, the worship of the church was enhanced by the gift of this new liturgy.[21]

In the General Preface to the new Prayer Book I wrote the following words:

> "Is liturgical revision an offensive luxury at such a time as this? The answer is an emphatic 'no', because the Church's worship of God in prayer and sacrament is a priority in every circumstance, and very particularly in times of crisis and change....
>
> Liturgy becomes true worship when the people of God, clergy and laity, clothe it with the devotion of heart and mind. Then it becomes a flame, kindled and re-kindled by the Holy Spirit, for our benefit and for God's glory. What is more, worship releases into the world, with its need and its pain, its sorrow and its hope, an influence for healing and wholeness which we shall never fully comprehend....
>
> It is in this spirit that this Prayer Book is offered for use in these times, which, though daunting, yet quicken our faith in the living God."[22]

Love for God: love for neighbour. These are two sides of the same coin. The true chapel of the heart embraces both.

Thirteen – Endnotes

1   Henri Nouwen: *Gracias! – Diary of a Latin American Pilgrimage,* (Orbis Books, New York, 1993), page 172.

2   John Allen (ed.): *The Essential Desmond Tutu* (David Philip, Cape Town, 1997), pages 76-78.

3   Ibid, page 7.

4   Sally du Plessis: *My Favourite Room – Desmond Tutu* in *The Sunday Star Magazine,* 23 December 1990.

5   Ibid. 'Ja' is the Afrikaans for 'Yes', often used colloquially in South Africa when English is being spoken.

6   Ibid.

7   This phrase is adapted from the writings of Brother Lawrence, the 17th century spiritual writer. See Brother Lawrence: *The Practice of the Presence of God* (Translated by E M Blaiklock) (Hodder and Stoughton, London et al, 1981), page 41. "We can make a chapel of our heart, to which we can from time to time withdraw...."

8   Luke 1: 68-79.

9   *The Official Report of the Lambeth Conference, 1998,* (Morehouse Publishing, 1999), page 33, a quotation from *The Virginia Report of the Inter-Anglican Theological and Doctrinal Commission.*

10 See Lawrence Schlemmer and Elda Susan Morroen: *Faith for the Fearful? An Investigation into new churches in the Greater Durban Area* (Centre for Applied Social Sciences, University of Natal, 1984).

11 Michael Harper (ed.): *Bishops' Move* (Hodder and Stoughton, London et al, 1978), page 31. Bill Burnett contributed an important essay to this book entitled *The Spirit and Social Action* (pages 29-59).

12 Bill Bendyshe Burnett: *The Rock that is Higher than I* (Sheila Burnett, Grahamstown, 1997), page 182.

13 John 1: 12.

14 Genesis 1: 26-27.

15 This is the title of a book by Sheldon Vanauken.

16 Julian of Norwich: *Revelations of Divine Love* (Penguin,

1998), page 83.

17 *Anglican Update*, Vol. 1, No. 9, October 1994.

18 Ibid.

19 Ibid.

20 These were Afrikaans, Sesotho, Xhosa and Zulu.

21 For a fuller account, see Michael Nuttall: *A river running through – liturgical life and change in the CPSA* in John Suggit and Mandy Goedhals (eds.): *Change and Challenge – Essays commemorating the 150th anniversary of the arrival of Robert Gray as first bishop of Cape Town* (CPSA, 1998), pages 55-62.

22 See *An Anglican Prayer Book 1989 – Church of the Province of Southern Africa* (Collins, London, 1989), pages 9-11.

Chapter Fourteen

Icon of Reconciliation

"Beloved country of grief and grace." (Antjie Krog)[1]

In October 1994, during the week of his 63rd birthday, Desmond let it be known in a newspaper interview that he was exhausted and looking forward to his retirement in 1996.[2] Yet he did not cease to be fully engaged with the affairs of both church and state. Indeed, while warmly welcoming the newly elected government and praising it for much in its early performance, he did not hesitate to criticise the size of the salaries being drawn by parliamentarians and government ministers. He also sharply questioned the promotion by the government of an arms trade that he felt would undermine the new South Africa's high moral ground.

At the Provincial Synod in Kimberley in September 1995 Desmond once again looked to the future and his coming retirement. In his Charge he said: "It is right that a change of leadership should happen now. We have been involved very much in the *against* mode, fighting against apartheid. Our countries have entered a new phase in their histories when the emphasis must be on building, on constructing, on developing, on healing – very much a *for* mode. You need new energy, a fresh vision, new insights...What a privilege to be able to hand over this vibrant, tingling going concern to my successor. God be praised, for the Church belongs to God."[3]

It was at the Synod of Bishops, immediately before this Provincial Synod, that an unexpected turn of events occurred which held out a whole new prospect for Desmond and for the South African nation. Desmond himself describes what happened in his penetrating book, *No Future Without Forgiveness*:

> "I thought I was about to retire as Archbishop when in September 1995 my penultimate meeting of our synod of bishops unanimously nominated me to the President for membership of the Truth and Reconciliation Commission. I was one of about forty-five who made the shortlist from an original list of approximately 200 nominations. We were interviewed by a multi-party panel in public hearings held in several centres of South Africa. The panel sent twenty-five names to the President who, in consultation with the cabinet of his Government of National Unity, chose seventeen people to be the new Truth and Reconciliation Commission. I was appointed chairperson, with Dr Alex Boraine as the Deputy Chair.
>
> When the President requests, then lesser mortals have little option. Who could say no to Mr Mandela? My much-longed-for break went out of the window. For nearly three years we would be involved in the devastating but also exhilarating work of the Commission, listening to the harrowing tales of horrendous atrocities and being uplifted by the extraordinary generosity of spirit of so many of our compatriots. It was an incredible privilege."[4]

Behind the unanimous nomination by the Synod of Bishops in September 1995 lay a story in which I had played an intriguing part. On 23 July Desmond and I were present, with many others, at a service in St Mary's Cathedral, Johannesburg – the very cathedral where he had served as both Dean and Bishop – to celebrate with another former Bishop of Johannesburg, Leslie Stradling, the fiftieth anniversary of his episcopal consecration. It was a glorious occasion, full of the rich worship that often characterises and sustains the life of the CPSA. I had been much in thought, during the preceding weeks, about a growing conviction that I should put before Desmond the possibility of allowing his name to be considered for the forthcoming Truth and Reconciliation Commission. I had learnt to be careful about giving him advice or expressing an opinion, because very often he acted on it immediately, sometimes almost impulsively. I knew that he was exhausted and looking forward to his retirement, for which he and his wife, Leah, had well-laid plans for a long sabbatical at Emory University in Atlanta. Apart from the welcome rest and the opportunity to teach which this would give him, they would be able to spend quality time with their daughters, sons-in-law and grandchildren who live in the United States. It seemed unfair to make any kind of intrusion upon this prospect.

Yet was it right to disobey what seemed to be one of those 'divine nudges' about which Desmond himself sometimes spoke? Was it truly a nudge, or was it a figment of my own imagination? In the vestry before the service began, I told him that I had something I wished to talk with him about and that I would be glad of an opportunity when the service was over. I knew that he was leaving immediately after the service, in his capacity as President of the All-Africa Conference of Churches, for an important commitment in Rwanda, following the terrible genocide in that country. I also knew that there might not be a similar face-to-face opportunity for quite a while. In the event it proved impossible to speak to him because, at the end of the service, he was mobbed by members of the congregation and then had to be rushed to the airport. I decided to speak instead to John Allen who was going to be travelling with him. "John", I said, "please will you say to the Arch (our nickname for him) that I cannot get out of my mind the thought that he should consider letting himself be nominated for membership of the Truth and Reconciliation Commission? I have hesitated because I know of his retirement plans. But think of what he might be missing! He would also be ideal for the job." John did speak to 'the Arch', and the reply was negative; he thought that 'new blood' was needed not only in the church but in the affairs of the nation as well. I said nothing more, and was surprised by joy when, just before the beginning of the Synod of Bishops in September, he took me aside and said that he and Leah had been pondering and praying over the suggestion and had now come to the conclusion that he should allow his name to go forward. This change of mind was conveyed very quietly, almost as if he was still praying about it, and I became even more aware of the cost. So it was that I was able, with Desmond's permission, to raise my proposal with all the bishops. Without any hesitation we made our unanimous nomination to President Nelson Mandela in a letter signed by each of us individually.

The fertile role of the Truth and Reconciliation Commission is now a well-known part of recent South African history. It was the nation's catharsis as both victims and perpetrators of gross human rights violations in the apartheid era came to the Commission's public hearings to tell their searing stories. The victims – or survivors, to give them a nobler and more dignified title – were entitled to receive reparation from the state. The perpetrators, if their crimes were politically motivated and they made full disclosure, were entitled to be given individual amnesty. There were those South Africans who would have preferred to see a just punishment of perpetrators through the courts. One of the problems with this, as has happened in certain cases where prosecutions have occurred, is the provision of sufficient evidence to secure a conviction beyond reasonable doubt. Quite apart from this difficulty, the rationale behind the TRC was to take the nation beyond retributive justice into the realm of mercy on the other side of truth telling. Through this process, information on a dark and sinister era, which may not otherwise have come to light, emerged voluntarily. It was this truth, told by both victims and perpetrators, which made genuine reconciliation a possibility.

The work of the TRC has evoked enormous interest in other parts of the world where there has been similar conflict and gross violation of human rights. It has held out the picture of a nation of wounded healers, facing its past lest that past come back to haunt it, looking to the future as a forgiven and forgiving community. These have been the essences of 'truth' and 'reconciliation', two extremely difficult ideals to effect in personal relationships, let alone the relationships of a whole nation which has been torn apart. Our truth and reconciliation process, led by the work of the Commission, has not been perfect. It was hindered by the sceptical, the hostile and the indifferent, and also by the lack of full disclosure from some of the participants in the process. We were dealing, as always, with fragile and fallible human beings. Yet, in spite of these drawbacks, the TRC accomplished its healing task in a remarkable way, and there can be little doubt that this was due in no small measure to the grace, wisdom and deep humanity of its leader.

I like to think that probably the most important thing I did in my seven years as Dean of the Province in the CPSA, taking the full perspective of our tortured yet liberating history into account, was to plant that seed into the mind and heart of a reluctant yet resilient Archbishop. I have already mentioned that I was ordained priest on one of the festivals of John the Baptist, who was uniquely the preparer of the way for the coming of Jesus. Many times in the life of the church I found myself fulfilling a similar role: preparing or easing the way for another, being the 'number two'. Here perhaps was the most notable example of it. When Desmond was formally appointed to chair the Commission I wrote to him as follows:

"My dear Desmond

You were in the USA when the Nobel Peace Prize came your way and also when the bishopric of Johannesburg came your way, and now when the chairing of the Truth and Reconciliation Commission has come your way. What is it about the United States that is so special?

Thank you for responding as you did to the original 'nudge'. I am deeply aware of the personal sacrifice which you – and Leah – have made. I can only say, in expressing gratitude, that I am sure God will use this to enhance and strengthen the healing of our land. I congratulate you warmly on the appointment. It shows the President's – and others' – confidence in you for this very sensitive and significant work....

For my part I shall do all I can to help relieve you of Archiepiscopal pressures and responsibilities which you will clearly not be able to handle in the first six months of 1996."[5]

With Alex Boraine as Deputy Chair of the TRC, Desmond found himself with a fresh 'number two'. It is evident from Boraine's published work on the Commission that they worked closely and happily together. "I had known Desmond Tutu for more than thirty years but hadn't worked with him very closely. He is a man of many gifts and graces, and with his genial, embracing manner he quickly put all of us at ease."[6] Yet there were some relational problems in the Commission at the beginning. About its very first meeting Boraine writes: "...There was strong evidence of his (Tutu's) episcopal authority, which was very quickly challenged. It didn't take him too long to realise that he wasn't dealing with a group of priests or even bishops, but some independent-minded and quite often difficult people."[7] It is true that deference to religious authority is strong, probably too strong, in the church, and that bishops can wield their power, including their power of persuasion, without sufficient challenge. Perhaps Desmond had it too easy among his colleagues in the church. What is not true, however, is to imagine that there are no independent-minded or difficult people among priests and bishops! With sensitivity and skill, and some obvious adaptation, Desmond had no alternative but to start all over again, as he had done in 1986, with the building of a vibrant team.

Boraine's final judgment on Tutu's role in the TRC is unequivocal. "There were other South Africans who could have served equally well on the Commission. With one exception. I don't think the Commission could have survived without the presence and person of Desmond Tutu....His choice by President Mandela was an inspired one. He assisted the Commission enormously in every possible way to become an instrument for healing, perhaps because he always saw himself and his colleagues on the Commission as wounded healers, not better than anyone else, but simply people who had been given a job to do and who cared very deeply for victims and perpetrators alike."[8]

In January 1997, a year after the TRC began its work, Desmond was diagnosed with prostate cancer. News of this left me shattered, not only because of the illness but because of the sense of responsibility I carried for suggesting that he allow himself to be considered for this stressful work. He had to leave the Commission for some months while he received treatment. Alex Boraine felt his absence deeply. "To manage and lead without him added considerably to the burden we normally faced together."[9] Desmond returned and made an even more profound impact. Boraine writes: "I think Tutu's illness affected him very deeply but in a strange way enabled him to guide and direct the work of the Commission with even greater sensitivity."[10] I need not have worried as much as I did. Instead, it became important to remember the words of St Paul: "God said to me, 'My grace is sufficient for you, for my power is made perfect in weakness.'"[11]

I had only one direct personal involvement, in November 1997, with the sittings of the TRC. It was also vicarious because Desmond's successor as Archbishop of Cape Town, Njongonkulu Ndungane, asked me to make the CPSA's presentation on his behalf at one of the 'religious hearings', when different churches and other faith communities had an opportunity to participate. Once again Desmond and I were thrown together. In my submission I made two references to him and his leadership during the apartheid years. First I touched on his key role in the church:

> "During the last eight years of the apartheid regime (1986-1994) our church was presided over, in its life and synodical government, by a

black archbishop who, by sheer example, demonstrated once and for all how crazy, let alone immoral, the alternative apartheid model was for our society. Yet this same archbishop – I hardly need to remind you, Chairperson! – did not have a vote in the land of his birth." [12]

I then referred to his much wider prophetic role:

"In the closing years of apartheid rule, the bishops of the CPSA resolved to appoint no more military chaplains. At about the same time, the call for economic sanctions – which you, Chairperson, had issued much earlier in a single-handed act of moral courage – was supported corporately by the bishops of the CPSA and, indeed, by its highest synod in 1989. It could be said – and I would include myself in this stricture – that we took too long to come to this place of a clearer, uncompromising witness. We allowed others to precede us and take the flak. Too late we conceded that they were right, and we owe them an apology for our compromising and often complacent half-heartedness, and sometimes for a hardness of heart that could be extremely damaging and hurtful. Archbishop, you yourself bore the brunt of this critique not only in the nation at large but even from the membership of your own church. May I, on behalf of the CPSA, offer you a profound apology, ask for your forgiveness, and thank you for your extraordinary graciousness and magnanimity?" [13]

These were moving moments for me, a catharsis, a recognition that our friendship was a gift of grace when so much around us could have made it an impossibility.

The Roman Catholic writer, Henri Nouwen, described love for neighbour memorably as a movement from hostility to hospitality.[14] This is one way of describing the essence of our country's history in the closing decade of the twentieth century. Old hostilities were being set aside in favour of a new inclusiveness where everyone counted and belonged. The Truth and Reconciliation Commission made a vitally important contribution to this process. It became another key feature in the undoing of conquest – the inward aspect – to which I referred in the Prologue to this book. Desmond Tutu joined Nelson Mandela in standing astride this period as a moral giant, icon of a costly, not a cheap, reconciliation.

Fourteen – Endnotes

1   Antjie Krog: *Country of my Skull* (Vintage, London et al, 1999), page 395.

2   Sam Sole: *That Troublesome Priest* in the *Sunday Tribune*, 2 October 1994.

3   *The Archbishop's Charge to Provincial Synod, Kimberley, September 1995*, pages 7-8.

4   Desmond Tutu: *No Future Without Forgiveness* (Rider, London et al, 1999), page 61.

5   Letter to Desmond, 4 December 1995.

6   Alex Boraine: *A Country Unmasked* (Oxford University Press, 2000), page 17.

7   Ibid, page 17.

8   Ibid, page 268.

9   Ibid, page 90.

10 Ibid, page 90. Another fine study of the TRC and its hearings, which the author attended as a representative of the South African Broadcasting Corporation, is Antjie Krog: *Country of my Skull* (Vintage, London et al, 1999).

11 2 Corinthians 12: 9.

12 Michael Nuttall: *A Submission to the Truth and Reconciliation Commission's Faith Community Hearings*, East London, 17-19 November 1997. See Appendix Two for this submission in full.

13 Ibid.

14 Henri J M Nouwen: *Reaching Out* (Collins, London, 1980), page 61.

Chapter Fifteen

Farewell to the Archbishop

"Good gracious – do we *realise* what has happened during this one short decade? Dear God, what would it have been like without him?" (Christopher Ahrends, Acting Dean of St George's Cathedral, Cape Town)[1]

Desmond remained 'de jure' Archbishop of Cape Town during the first seven months of the life of the Truth and Reconciliation Commission. One of the practical problems was that occasions to mark his retirement had been made well before his appointment to the TRC. It would not have been easy to persuade the Archbishop of Canterbury or President Mandela to make a sudden change in their diaries. Nor was it easy to alter the chosen date for one of the two venues, the Good Hope Centre in Cape Town, which had to be booked many months in advance. We decided to stay on course with our plans. Desmond continued to undertake what he could as Archbishop and to live at Bishopscourt, but in reality most tasks had to be performed by others. I personally began to feel the pinch of my original suggestion about Desmond and the TRC. For the first and last time I had to preside over a full, four-day session of the Synod of Bishops. I sent him a fax during the Synod in which I said: "We have been quite good in your absence, but we have been missing our ex-Headmaster enormously."[2] He replied: "I missed being with you all, but it was made easier knowing that you

would be in the Chair."[3]   A mutual trust had, over the
years, become self-evident.

Presiding over the Farewells Committee took a great
deal of time and energy, including regular flights from
Natal to Cape Town. I also represented the CPSA in
Parliament in May on the occasion of the acceptance of
South Africa's new Constitution, a remarkable document
which had taken two years to complete in the Constituent
Assembly under the joint presidency of Cyril Ramaphosa
of the African National Congress and Leon Wessels of the
National Party. In this same period, as has been previously
described, 'Project Ukuthula' was under way in KwaZulu-
Natal in preparation for the local government elections.
Church leaders and others were pushed to the limit in
their continuing quest for peace. Amazingly, Desmond
found time to come to Pietermaritzburg in March of that
year to spend two hours in the vigil area of the cathedral
to pray for peace.

There were two farewell services for him in June, and in
between these a new Archbishop of Cape Town was to be
elected. It was a month full of emotion and memory and
new expectation. Above all, it was a time of great
thanksgiving. The first service was a Eucharistic
celebration for the people of the church, in the diocese of
Cape Town, in the CPSA, and ecumenically. Desmond
preached his farewell sermon in both a moving and a
jocular way. "God," he said, "must have an excellent sense
of humour to appoint someone with a name like Tutu to
this position. I have inspired a graffiti which said 'I used to
be an Anglican until I put two-and-two together.'"[4]   He
invited all to work together to make 'God's dream' come
true for a more caring, more gentle, more compassionate
South Africa.

The second service, three weeks later, was a civic
service in St George's Cathedral attended by dignitaries
not only from Southern Africa but from all over the world.
It had been the same at his installation ten years before.
Then, it was to provide support for a brave and vulnerable
leader. Now, it was to pay tribute. We had confidentially
approached President Nelson Mandela to suggest a South

African civic award. At the service itself the President gave Desmond the highest award the nation could offer: the Order of Meritorious Service, Gold. It was the first time in his presidency that he had made such an award. Robert Runcie had come as Archbishop of Canterbury to Desmond's enthronement in 1986. Now, ten years later, his successor, George Carey, came to the farewell service and preached the sermon. In addition, Carey presented Desmond with a newly established award for outstanding

Desmond receives the Order of Meritorious Service
from President Nelson Mandela

service to the Anglican Communion.

It was my joy to offer the following prayers of thanksgiving at the service:

> "We thank you, God, for the ministry of leadership;
> for those you give to guide and inspire us,
> especially for Desmond, beloved bishop, Metropolitan and Nobel Laureate,
> for his vision, courage, energy, compassion and humour,
> for his spirituality so deeply rooted,
> for all the gifts you have given him and for all he has given to us.
> We thank you, God, for Desmond's ministry throughout the world,
> for hearts stirred and actions inspired,
> for hope restored and faith uplifted,
> for his commitment to peace and justice in the nearest and farthest corners of the earth,
> for his voice among the voiceless and marginalized."

Here we sought to touch the true source and nature of authentic ministry, and in our thanksgiving we acknowledged the God who calls and equips us for that work.

The bishops of the CPSA, on the evening before the first of these two farewell services, had arranged a dinner for Desmond and Leah. It was an occasion of much hilarity despite the solemnities that were also on our minds, Desmond's own exuberant humour making its accustomed contribution. But there came a moment which almost reduced him to tears, when on behalf of the bishops I announced our decision that, from 1 July 1996, he would be our 'Archbishop Emeritus'. Anglican archbishops, when they retire, normally revert to being 'Bishop'. Titles are not important, but we were aware that for most people Desmond would always be 'the Arch'. Already in the work of the TRC he was known as

*The procession leaves St George's Cathedral at the end of the
farewell service. Incense envelops the Tutu family and honoured
guests. In this photograph, from the lower left, are
Deputy President F W de Klerk, Deputy President Thabo Mbeki,
King Letsie III of Lesotho, President Joachim Chissano of
Mozambique, President Ketumile Masire of Botswana and
President Nelson Mandela. Immediately above Mandela's head
is Mrs Leah Tutu, and standing behind him is the
South African Chief Justice, Michael Corbett.*

Archbishop; it would be helpful for everyone if he kept the
title. In addition, it was our small but special way of being
able to honour him a little, our way of saying 'thank you'
for an exceptional ministry.

At the farewell Eucharist next day, it was my
responsibility to pay tribute to Desmond on behalf of the
CPSA as a whole. Frustratingly, the Farewells Committee
had given me only three minutes in which to do it! By the
time my wife and I flew to Cape Town from Durban, I had

still not decided finally how to go about it. Fortunately, on that aeroplane trip I experienced unexpectedly a rare spasm of poetic inspiration. Prose is my preferred style rather than poetry. Yet, on this occasion, could anything be said memorably in prose in a mere three minutes? One of our bishops, Itumeleng Moseki, when he was still a priest, had offered a traditional African 'praise song' in Tswana to Desmond at the end of the Provincial Synod in 1995. He had produced an English translation, and some of its phrases had teased my mind ever since. Using these as a springboard – and with acknowledgements to Itumeleng – I decided to offer my own version of a praise song:

HAIL
Small creature of the Western Transvaal,
where the gentle BaTswana and some hard people
live;
Raised in a humble teacher's home,
living in the shadow of the great injustice.

HAIL
Mfundisi, Moruti,[5]
Raised through sickness to a priestly calling,
finding the fire in your breast which prevented
silence:
Articulate scholar, prophet, pastor, pray-er,
preacher of passion with arms stretched out,
diminutive person making presidents tremble.
Small creature of the past becoming great
in the unfolding purposes of God.
Greetings, God's champion.

HAIL
Mbhishobhi[6]
Learning the art in mountain kingdom
being greeted 'Khotso, Ntate.'[7]
Learning the harder way in the land of gold,
learning the bitter irony of red carpets abroad
and icy stares back home,

learning to lean on God and drawing on the safety
valve of an irrepressible humour.

HAIL
Great creature, voice of the muted multitude,
son of the dark, mysterious land,
Called at the height of crisis to the Cape of Storms
to transform it into the Cape of Good Hope:
Greetings Mbhishobhi OMkhulu,[8]
with the fire still in your breast for liberation
of the oppressed and the oppressor,
for women and for the young:
'Called to labour with God to help God's children
become ever more fully human,
which is a glorious destiny'.

FAREWELL
Creature of the nation, archbishop of the people,
now called into a further costly way
towards truth and reconciliation
towards healing for us all.
Farewell, first among wounded healers.
Fare thee well, first among equals,
our Archbishop Emeritus from 1 July 1996.
Farewell, our friend and our brother,
to whom we are so deeply indebted.

Take rest, we pray, before too long,
Repair to the quiet shadows,
the haunt of your own illustrious forebears,
And there tend the wounds of noble strife.

Aah	Desmond Mpilo Tutu
	Mbhishobhi OMkhulu.
Aah	Leah Nomalizo Tutu,
	true Gogo[9] of the Province.
Aah	small creature who has become great
	in the service of God and God's people.
Aah	Amen.

We greet each other at Desmond's home, Bishopscourt,
after the farewell service.

Two days later, on 4 June 1996, with this farewell
occasion still ringing in our ears, I presided as Dean of the
Province over the Cape Town Elective Assembly for the
election of Desmond's successor. Almost exactly ten years
earlier Desmond and I had been the two candidates for
election. Now he was retired and well into his new work
with the Truth and Reconciliation Commission, and I was
just over three years away from retirement myself. Once
again, there were just two candidates, and once again the
Bishop of Johannesburg – Desmond's successor there,
Duncan Buchanan – was one of them. The other was
Njongonkulu Ndungane, Bishop of Kimberley and
Kuruman. Each was a distinguished son of the church,
rich in experience. Each had in his time been in charge of
one of the CPSA's theological colleges. As with Desmond
and me, there were also significant differences between
them in background, race and culture. The Elective

Assembly chose Ndungane, and thus the succession moved, in keeping with changing times, towards the new millennium.

I was ready by 1997 to be relieved of my role as Dean of the Province when Lawrence Zulu, the Bishop of Swaziland, was elected by the Synod of Bishops to replace me. Lawrence and I regarded each other as ecclesiastical twins, for we had been consecrated as bishops together on 16 November 1975. With his election, I was able to concentrate my energies more fully on my concluding years as Bishop of Natal until my retirement at the end of January, 2000. Yet, always, I would look back on my close partnership with Desmond Tutu as the 'anni mirabili', the wondrous years.

Fifteen – Endnotes

1   Christopher Ahrends in *Gateway*, magazine of St George's Cathedral, June 1996.

2   Fax to Desmond, 15 February 1996.

3   Letter to me, 27 March 1996.

4   *Cape Times*, 3 June 1996.

5   Two words for 'priest' or 'minister' in Zulu and Tswana respectively.

6   Meaning 'bishop' in Zulu.

7   Meaning 'Peace, Father' in Sesotho.

8   Meaning 'great bishop', that is, 'archbishop' in Zulu.

9   Meaning 'grandmother' in Zulu.

Soul Brothers [1]

The prophetic nature of Desmond Tutu's job as Archbishop of Cape Town will ensure that he remains a controversial figure. Nobel Laureate or not, his advocacy of sanctions against South Africa has not endeared him to the establishment, and some strong critics have even labelled him as "anti-Christ".

Yet it cannot be disputed that he remains a moderate, even reasonable voice, in the general political cacophony. Is the fact that he doesn't appeal to all not simply a consequence of his vocation – and perhaps his race?

The role of a black leader in South Africa today demands courage. And if that leader's constituency is split between black and white, how much more difficult could that role be?

As voices in the Anglican Church are raised against him, and funds from dedicated givers seem to dwindle, there is clearly another side of the matter to consider.

Why did his Brothers in Christ elect Desmond Tutu to be their leader – and with such enthusiasm?

On the eve of Tutu's enthronement as Archbishop, Leadership asked Michael Nuttall to address this vexed question.

His answer is all the more meaningful since it was Nuttall, as Bishop of Natal, who posed the only serious alternative to the election of Tutu. He was also the choice of the Anglican establishment.

"Most Reverend Father in God, we present unto you this godly and well-learned man to be ordained and consecrated Bishop."

These are the words used by the two presenting bishops when they present a priest to the archbishop to be consecrated. It is a solemn moment.

Desmond Mpilo Tutu was consecrated bishop on 11

July 1976 in St Mary's Cathedral, Johannesburg. I had the privilege of being one of his presenting bishops, for he had kindly asked me to act in this way. At the time I was a very new bishop myself, having been Bishop of Pretoria for less than a year. Desmond was Dean (the first black dean) of Johannesburg. We had come to know each other some years before when he was a lecturer at the Federal Theological Seminary at Alice and I was a lecturer at Rhodes University in Grahamstown. Now we were to be brother bishops, for he had been elected to be Bishop (the first black bishop) of Lesotho.

I was close enough to notice that Bishop Desmond was visibly moved on the day of his consecration. What were the thoughts, I wondered, jostling in his alert and active mind? What were the emotions tugging at his warm and sensitive heart? July 11, 1976 was within a month of 'Soweto 1976' – that landmark which would change the course of South Africa's history.

Only a month or so before the events in Soweto and elsewhere, Desmond had written during a three-day retreat his now famous letter to Prime Minister John Vorster pleading with him to offer some meaningful signs of change. Let urban black people become permanent, with freehold rights. Let the pass laws be repealed.[2] Let a national convention of genuine leaders be called together. These were the moderate requests he made.

> "I am writing to you, Sir, because I have a growing nightmarish fear that unless something is done very soon, then bloodshed and violence are going to happen in South Africa almost inevitably. A people can take only so much and no more."

Such were his prophetic words in May 1976.

Two months later this leader was being strangely taken to a remote mountainous place, far away from the scene of action. What could God and his church be up to? Desmond had been Dean of Johannesburg for two short years. How was one to understand the surprises of God?

It turned out that Bishop Desmond was not to be long in Lesotho either. After only another two years he accepted, with the approval of his brother bishops, the position of General Secretary of the South African Council of Churches. Thus he came back in March 1978 to his beloved Johannesburg for seven turbulent, decisive and formative years both in his own life and ministry and in the life of church and nation.

The time in Lesotho was important: a refining, waiting time. Desmond knew the country already, for he had taught for a spell in earlier years at Roma University. Now he was there in a new capacity, away for a brief spell from the full glare of publicity in the Republic. There were inevitably the calls back to South Africa – for Steve Biko's immense funeral in Kingwilliamstown, for example, in 1977. Desmond delivered a powerful oration, once again pleading for peaceful change before it was too late:

"We cry for our beloved country which has been so wanton in its waste of her precious human resources."

Bishop Desmond has always said that he is first and foremost a pastor, and it is true that within the prophet's cry for justice there lies a pastoral concern for people, both the oppressed and the oppressor. In Lesotho there was plenty of scope for the pastor, visiting, caring, nurturing the flock even in the remotest parts which can only be reached on horseback. Moreover, Desmond's time in Lesotho gave him a Southern African experience and perspective which will stand him in good stead now as he begins to preside over the affairs of the Church of the Province of Southern Africa, comprising Mozambique, Swaziland, Lesotho and Namibia as well as the parts traditionally known as South Africa. He is the third South African-born Archbishop of Cape Town, the other two being Bill Burnett and Philip Russell. He is the first Archbishop who has been bishop in his time of a part of the Province which is not in South Africa. That in itself is a good and healthy development.

So it was that Desmond came back to Johannesburg in 1978. As a bishop of the Church it must in many ways have been a lonely time at the SACC, not having a diocese and therefore not being a member of the Synod of Bishops.

Eventually he longed to come back into diocesan ministry, the true ministry of a bishop. Yet it was supremely during his years as General Secretary of the SA Council of Churches that he emerged as a person not only of national but of international stature. Ironically, the South African government contributed to this through its relentless pursuit of the policy of apartheid and through its particular assault on the SACC as one of its more implacable opponents.

When Bishop Bill Burnett had been Secretary of the SACC (or Christian Council of South Africa, as it was then called) *The Message to the People of South Africa* had been produced with its theological critique of an ideology which made racial identity rather than a person's humanity the essential guideline to government policy. Desmond Tutu did not invent a new critique; he simply carried through the old and existing one, but with a passion and tenacity which made everyone sit up and take note. He showed no fear in the face of a government that possessed, and still possesses, immense power. He would say, after St Paul:

"If God is for us, who can be against us?"

The plight of the many thousands who were subjected to forced removal from their homes touched, in a particular way, his heart of righteous anger and compassion. Often he has told the story of the small girl he met in a resettlement camp who, when he asked what she did to stave off hunger pains, said: "I drink water." He could not, and cannot, forget the face of that child. Here we see the heart and mind of prophet and pastor blending in a fierce yet tender care.

The climax for Bishop Desmond at the SACC was the Eloff Commission of Enquiry into the affairs of the organization and his own testimony before the commission. The testimony has been published under the title of *The Divine Intention*, in which he defended the truths he holds dear, both in the Scriptures and in what he attractively calls "the hallowed Christian tradition". What is the divine intention for us?

"Our Lord has tried to weld us into a family: people of different races, who demonstrate,

however feebly and fitfully, what this beautiful
land can be. If only we could begin to treat people
as persons created by God in His image,
redeemed by Jesus Christ and sanctified by the
Holy Spirit. What a wonderful land it could be...."
Here was Tutu the Christian idealist, speaking words
reminiscent of the 19th century Anglican theologian, F D
Maurice, who said: "You are brothers; you must become
what you are." The prophetic voice was also evident:

"There is nothing the government can do to
me that will stop me from being involved in what
I believe is what God wants me to do. I do not do
it because I like doing it....I cannot help it when I
see injustice. I will not keep quiet, for, as
Jeremiah says, when I try to keep quiet, God's
word burns like a fire in my breast. But what is it
that they can ultimately do? The most awful thing
that they can do is to kill me, and death is not the
worst thing that can happen to a Christian."

Strong words. Brave words. Words before which one has
little alternative but to be silent; words reminiscent of
Martin Luther when he stood before the Emperor Charles
V and said: "Here I stand, I can do no other; so help me,
God."

The Nobel Peace Prize was a symbol of the outside
world's response. It was a personal award, but Desmond
received it and welcomed it as a vicarious award also; it
was for him a vindication of the SACC. He was the second
South African to receive the award. In some ways one
cannot think of two more different personalities than
Albert Luthuli and Desmond Tutu: the one grave,
aristocratic and for good reason known and loved as 'the
Chief'; the other a self-made man, born in a Transvaal
township and through sheer pluck and effort making good,
and finally finding himself in the unenviable glare of
international glitter and publicity. Yet, with their
differences of character and background, each has
pursued out of deep Christian conviction the same ideals
amidst the same obstacles, and nearly forty years of
apartheid have at least achieved this: they have given us

two Nobel Peace Prize winners in a single generation!

There could easily have been a third, but his is a different link with Norway in that it was there, in a hotel bedroom, that he wrote the opening chapter of an immortal book called *Cry, the Beloved Country.*

Bishop Desmond was on a sabbatical in New York when the bishops of the Church of the Province, meeting at Modderpoort in the Orange Free State in November 1984, chose him to succeed Timothy Bavin as Bishop of Johannesburg. It was Timothy Bavin who had appointed him Dean of Johannesburg ten years earlier. His career now came full circle as, once again, he entered St Mary's Cathedral, this time to occupy the bishop's chair. At his enthronement in February 1985 he said: "I hope to end my ministry as bishop of Johannesburg." That was an understandable hope. At the same time, having experienced the surprises of God before in his life, he knew that he could not make this hope a cast-iron condition, and so he added the words "unless it becomes abundantly clear that God wills me to do otherwise".

It became abundantly clear on Monday, 14 April 1986 when he was elected to be Archbishop of Cape Town. Elective assemblies are not, of course, infallible vehicles of the divine will; they too can err because they are human. But the clarity and speed of the decision in Cape Town gave it a special flavour. It was a momentous day in the life of the church. Bishop Desmond was over-awed by the result. Who would not be? Yet his puckish humour, so well known to his friends and acquaintances, did not leave him. "I'm speechless," he said, " and I guess there are some who would prefer me to remain that way!" He also said something more searching and profound. Aware of his limitations and of the controversy which surrounds him, he said: "Please do not be angry with God because of me."

Bishop Desmond's election to be Archbishop is an important statement for us all. It is a symbol of what can be, of what must be, and of what is yet to be in our wayward church and nation. He stands for the many who need to be listened to at last and taken seriously. He stands also for a new style of leadership which will not necessarily follow Western norms. After all, he is African, and often he will speak and act and lead out of his African-ness.

But, above all, he is Christian, and it will be as a Christian disciple that he will seek to lead and serve. I heard him say at a conference a couple of years ago: "PW Botha is my brother". When subsequent speakers referred to the State President, they described him as 'Bishop Desmond's brother'! Twice, since his election as Archbishop, Desmond has had lengthy discussions with the State President. It cannot have been easy for him. There will be those who think he was wasting his time. Others will see him as a key mediator with credibility at both ends of the political scale. The truth is that it is as brothers and sisters that South Africans need to find solutions together to their country's problems.

Bishop Desmond demonstrates his brotherly spirit in a special way linguistically. His English is so accomplished that it is hard to remember that it is not his mother tongue. He also speaks Xhosa, Tswana, Sotho, Zulu and Afrikaans. Does not this versatility tell its own story? We can be thankful that we have a black Archbishop who was elected representatively by black and white alike and who gladly and willingly accepts responsibility for all. Does that not send a signal of hope to the land?

The Anglican Church prides itself with some justification on what it calls its comprehensiveness. Normally this applies to its understanding of Christian truth and doctrine. We like to think that we can hold together a variety of emphases and convictions within the one perimeter of truth. Sometimes this can get out of hand, when (for example) a bishop or a theologian goes off at a tangent which threatens to break the circle. But on the whole we tend to be tolerant of difference, recognising that no one possesses a monopoly of the truth. Certainly on difficult ethical questions we prefer not to be over-dogmatic, whether it be on issues like abortion or taking part in war or the advocating of sanctions; we recognise and allow for differences of emphasis and conviction on such things. Conscientious people are bound to differ in their ethical responses, especially when they are faced with choosing the lesser of two evils. They will also be influenced by their circumstances, for not even decisions of conscience are made in a social vacuum.

The principle of comprehensiveness can also apply in other directions, including political affiliation or preference and different kinds of leadership. It comes as a surprise to many that Oliver Tambo, Winnie Mandela and Chief Mangosuthu Buthelezi are all Anglicans. Despite its many failures, the church has done its work well over the years. A tapestry has emerged, reflecting the rich and varied life of our society. We are, to use a more human image, a family.

Out of that family God has raised a son to be his servant as Archbishop in these critical days. Bishop Desmond would no doubt have preferred it to be otherwise; he finds it heart-rending (to use his own word) to be leaving Johannesburg. But a new South Africa, and therefore a new Southern Africa, is coming to birth amidst much pain and travail. "The darkest hour, they say, is before the dawn." So spoke Desmond Tutu at Steve Biko's funeral.

This dynamic, diminutive man has made himself available because others asked that he should, to be a light in the darkness and to help lead us into the dawn of a new day. May he be given divine strength and wisdom for the task. His election to be Archbishop of Cape Town will be viewed by historians as a crossroads.

Appendix One – Endnotes

1   An article first published in *Leadership*, 1986, Number Four, pages 124-128. Reproduced here with permission.

2   Every black man and woman over the age of sixteen was required by law to carry at all times a passbook. It was popularly and derisively known as a 'dompass', the word 'dom' being the Afrikaans for 'stupid' or 'senseless'. If at any time the police discovered a person without a passbook, immediate arrest followed. This discriminatory identity document was a major symbol of oppression in South Africa.

Appendix Two

A Submission to the Truth and Reconciliation Commission [1]

Chairperson, I count it an awesome privilege to address you and other members of the Truth and Reconciliation Commission. I do so on behalf of, and at the request of, the Anglican Archbishop of Cape Town, Njongonkulu Ndungane, who is unfortunately not able to be present here today.

The Church of the Province of Southern Africa (CPSA) has made a written submission to the TRC, dated 30 June 1997. I ask for my remarks to be received as an amplification of that submission. Responsibility for these remarks is entirely my own.

I begin with a clarifying and explanatory point. The Church which I represent has within its title the phrase 'Southern Africa' because it embraces within its life and structure the countries of Angola, Lesotho, Mozambique, Namibia, Swaziland and the English dependency of St Helena, as well as the Republic of South Africa. All of these countries, with the possible exception of St Helena, have been caught up in their different and often exceedingly painful ways in the policy of apartheid, and it is with all of them in mind that this submission is being made. We need to be concerned about healing, reconciliation and reconstruction not only within South Africa itself, but also in neighbouring countries where South Africa fought its wars, created serious destabilisation, and drew on migrant labour. Many of the millions of landmines lying in the soil of Angola and Mozambique are a telling and terrible reminder of that process in the apartheid period. It seems to me that the churches which straddle these national frontiers in the Southern African region can play their part in promoting healing, reconciliation and reconstruction, in partnership with governments and others, in this subcontinent.

Chairperson, it is well known, I think, that the Church I represent was clear in its official and public condemnation of apartheid, eventually joining those who declared it to be a heresy and a sin. These pronouncements came from our synodical structure of church government in which black and white Anglicans participated together, providing an alternative model in our race-ridden society, which helped to point the way to the model of true democracy which our country has at last embraced. During the last eight years of the apartheid regime (1986 - 1994) our Church was presided over, in its life and synodical government, by a black Archbishop who, by sheer example, demonstrated once and for all how crazy, let alone immoral, the alternative apartheid model was for our society. Yet this same Archbishop - I need hardly remind you, Chairperson! - did not have a vote in the land of his birth.

But the picture I have just painted of our Church, though true, is far too rosy. The whole truth contains compromise, complacency and complicity alongside examples, on the part of some individuals, of great courage and compassion. The fact of the matter - as our written submission makes clear - is that the membership of the CPSA is varied and complex. Within the perspective of the TRC it includes a clear majority - some two million people - who were victims of apartheid, and a minority who were its beneficiaries, including some who were even its perpetrators. I well remember a synod resolution in which it was decided that any Anglican who was in the security police could not be elected to serve on a parish council. The opposition to this decision in some quarters of our Church was immediate.

Yet we did allow for the appointment of Anglican priests

as military chaplains to minister to the pastoral needs of white conscripts and professionals in the South African Defence Force. This came to be a deeply divisive issue in our Church, with parents of conscripts complaining bitterly that we did not have enough chaplains to minister to their sons, and black Anglicans bitterly opposed to having any chaplains at all. In our diocese of Namibia there was the particular embarrassment where the bishop there could not possibly approve of South African military chaplains coming to support what he and his people perceived to be an army of occupation. The liberation movements were also supported pastorally by Anglican priests, the difference being that they were not officially appointed to that role by the CPSA.

Here we touch on the difficult and sometimes painful interface between the pastoral and the prophetic in the life and witness of the church. How does the church achieve the balance between these two? In the closing years of apartheid rule, the bishops of the CPSA resolved to appoint no more military chaplains. At about the same time, the call for economic sanctions - which you, Chairperson, had issued much earlier in a single-handed act of moral courage - was supported corporately by the bishops of the CPSA and, indeed, by its highest synod in 1989. It could be said - and I would include myself in this stricture - that we took too long to come to this place of a clearer, uncompromising witness. We allowed others to precede us and take the flak. Too late we conceded that they were right, and we owe them an apology for our compromising and often complacent half-heartedness, and sometimes for a hardness of heart that could be extremely damaging and hurtful. Archbishop, you yourself bore the brunt of this critique not only in the nation at large but even from the membership of your own Church. May I, on behalf of the CPSA, offer you a profound apology, and ask for your forgiveness, and thank you for your extraordinary graciousness and magnanimity? May I also, through you, extend a similar message to all our other prophets, both within the Anglican Church and beyond it, thanking them for their courageous witness in the name of Christ to the truth?

Chairperson, paragraph 10 of the CPSA's written submission says that 'the CPSA acknowledges that there were occasions when, through the silence of its leadership or its parishes, or their actions in acquiescing with apartheid laws where they believed it to be in the interests of the Church, deep wrong was done to those who bore the brunt of the onslaught of apartheid'. What aided and abetted this kind of moral lethargy and acquiescence was the fact that, in many respects, our Church had developed over many years its own pattern of racial inequality and discrimination. It was all too easy to pass resolutions or make lofty pronouncements condemning apartheid. It was all too easy to point a morally superior finger at Afrikaner nationalist prejudice and pride. English pride and prejudice were no less real and were never very far below the surface of our high-sounding moral pronouncements. The Anglican Lord Milner must be as problematic to Afrikaner Christians as DF Malan the dominee[2] is to us. In a strange way I think many white Anglicans in the CPSA owe an apology to the Afrikaner community for their attitude of moral superiority. I became aware of this need when, as Bishop of Pretoria from 1976 – 1981, I got to know such fine Afrikaner Christians as David Bosch and Piet Meiring. Perhaps, Chairperson, I could ask Professor Piet Meiring in his capacity as a member of the TRC,[3] kindly to receive this expression of apology from a bishop of 'die Engelse kerk'.[4]

But our chief expression of apology must be to our own black membership, and I am using the word 'black' inclusively. Here we are speaking of the overwhelming majority of the CPSA, both in Southern Africa as a whole and in South Africa particularly. Interestingly, our black membership increased significantly in the early apartheid years, especially on the reef[5] where the witness against the new ideology was strong. Ours is primarily a black Church and it has been, and still is in many ways, a suffering Church: suffering at the hands of the Church itself.

Chairperson, our so-called white parishes, like white businesses (I am thinking of last week's TRC hearings),[6] have unquestionably benefited from apartheid and its political predecessors. In their church facilities, including housing and transport for their priests, they have been bastions of relative privilege. So-called black parishes, by contrast, like black businesses, have been decidedly disadvantaged in these respects. Within the black Anglican community there has been a further disparity in that, very often, as in the secular apartheid scenario, the African Church has been worse off than the Coloured,[7] and the Coloured Church worse off than the Indian. We have simply reflected the economic and social disparities at large. There was a time when even clergy stipends were paid on a racially different basis, with all kinds of clever justifications produced for what was essentially an ethically unacceptable practice.

Attempts are now being made to rectify these long-standing inequities within the life of our Church. Black advancement into leadership roles has been significant, but still within our Church's structures we are significantly dependent on white skill and expertise which can easily look and feel like white power blocking the aspirations of black people. A transformation process is under way, spearheaded by a recently created Black Anglican Forum. This will promote and facilitate an adjustment process for the CPSA as it moves into the new millennium, seeking to provide a new authenticity for our life together as a Church, setting us free to be more truly African in the broadest sense, to engage in our mission and ministry in a more authentic incarnational way.

Chairperson, this is one of the ways in which our denomination sees its commitment to the future of this country and this sub-continent: to be a transformed Church, under God, serving a transformed society. Central to that task will be our desire to contribute to a continuing process of healing and costly, not cheap, reconciliation. I speak as a church leader in a Province which has seen well over 15 000 politically motivated killings in a decade of traumatic transition. The healing of the resultant wounds, let alone the other wounds which are the legacy of apartheid, will engage the faith communities and others for a long time to come. One of the things which the KwaZulu-Natal Church Leaders' Group is planning for 1998 is a series of pastoral visits to 'places of pain' where, in the company of local communities, liturgies of healing and cleansing will occur, and symbolic actions will take place to facilitate reconciliation. Similarly, trauma workshops and workshops on repentance and restitution are available in our Province to enable people, bruised by a divided past, to come together in a wholesome, healing atmosphere in the presence of skilled facilitators, to find new hope for their lives.

Chairperson, I end with a final reflection or meditation on facets of the life of the CPSA which I represent here today, which I dearly love, and for whose failings and frailties I repent before God and this Commission.

- I think of the mother church, St George's Cathedral in Cape Town, site of faithful witness and struggle over many years, beacon of hope to the people alongside the Parliament where so many draconian laws were passed.

- I think, by contrast, of the faithful in Sekukuneland going on annual pilgrimage to the gravesite, at the top of a hill, of Manche Masemola, their martyr and ours.

- I think of the elderly member of the great Mothers' Union coming forward, slowly and painstakingly, to receive a certificate in honour of her 50 years' membership; and I hear her responding in grateful thanksgiving by singing in shaky voice a hymn from the depths of her being.

- I think of a small child coming forward to be confirmed -"Defend, O Lord, this thy child..." - and how I am struck by the innocence of her eyes and her folded hands.

- I think of a colleague as a teenager taking his critically ill father to hospital unaware that he would be refused admission because it was the white man's hospital, and going to another 'acceptable' hospital where there was only room for his father to lie on the floor, there to die a short while later; I think of this colleague carrying his pain into adult life, into the Black Consciousness Movement where he found his dignity affirmed, and finally finding healing when as a priest he was asked to be rector of a white congregation.

- I think of our present Archbishop incarcerated as a young man for three years as a political prisoner on Robben Island, and there finding his vocation to be a priest.

- I think of Zeph Mothopeng[8] standing up as a brave young man in Synod in the early apartheid years and challenging unsuccessfully the unequal stipends paid to clergy.

- I think of Trevor Huddleston's *Naught For Your Comfort*, and the costly intercessory prayer of the monks and the nuns, fighting apartheid on their knees, yearning for a new freedom to come.

- I think of those who understood none of these things, who were lost in their own limitations, trapped in their own small world.

- I think, and I think, and as I do so, I say 'Lord, have mercy', 'Nkosi, sihawukele', 'Morena, re gaugele', 'Kyrie, eleison'.[9] And then I say also 'Thank you, God, for your faithful ones, those who were clear-sighted, those who endured against all the odds to the end'.

Appendix Two – Endnotes

1   This was made at the Faith Community Hearings of the Truth and Reconciliation Commission in East London on 17 November 1997.

2   This is an Afrikaans word for a minister of religion.

3   Professor Meiring was present as a Commissioner when this apology was made.

4   This was a phrase often used in Afrikaans-speaking circles, meaning 'the English church'.

5   This refers to the gold mining reef in and around Johannesburg.

6   These hearings were for members of the business community.

7   This is a term used for people of mixed race.

8   He became a prominent leader in the Pan African Congress.

9   The cry for mercy is given here in isiZulu, Sesotho and Greek as well as English.

Index